SUPER GENBA:

TEN THINGS JAPANESE COMPANIES MUST DO TO GAIN GLOBAL COMPETITIVENESS

Francis McInerney

2014

2

4

TABLE OF CONTENTS

6

Super Genba:

Introduction

Nearly a quarter century ago, Japanese industry went into a tailspin. The Nikkei now trades roughly where it did in November 1984 when the Dow was at 1,200 and at a fifth of its peak at the close of 1989. This puts the Nikkei at about eight percent of what it would be today if it had tracked the Dow for the last thirty years. In what is the greatest stock market collapse in history, Japanese equity markets have been wiped out. Once-great Japanese export powerhouses that led their industries in innovation are today awash in losses and stagger under collapses of market share as innovators from elsewhere pass them by. Many have earnings that have not recovered R&D expenses in decades.

Whole families of products that Japan once dominated like video and still cameras, music players, and cell phones have dissolved into non-Japanese products like Apple's iPhone, leaving Japanese producers with nothing to sell in foreign markets and, more of a problem, no one to whom to sell.

Two decades ago, Japanese wireless services and products led the world. NTT was the first to introduce the apps that now litter the faces of iPhones and Android phones the world over. NEC was a leader in computerizing the phone network. Yet these Japanese products and services were never successfully exported. Today no one in telecommunications anywhere mentions Japan, even in passing. Japan is not a factor.

In industrial markets worldwide, Japanese suppliers routinely lose to faster-moving competitors whose products may not be as good. Often, Japanese companies discover markets that their better-informed foreign competitors identified years before and have been exploiting profitably for some time.

Pillars of Japanese industry like vertical integration and the widespread product portfolios that were meant to mitigate risk and worked so well half a century ago now produce little in the way of added value for customers.

Japan plays almost no role whatever in the cloud, the greatest industrial shift since the printing press half a millennium ago.

The result, profits that should be flowing into Japan from all over the world, are not.

It doesn't take much to understand that this cannot go on. Something has to change. If Japan cannot reenergize its position in global markets, it will become a tiny and irrelevant Chinese satellite. Foreseeing this, in late 2001, over a decade ago, the late Koji Nishigaki, then CEO of NEC, invited me to address a gathering of several thousand of his customers at the Tokyo Big Sight to tell them about the findings of my recent book with Sean White, *FutureWealth* (St. Martins, 2000). Introducing me, he told his customers that his biggest fear was seeing his country caught between a surging China of 1.5 billion people and a re-invigorated United States of 300 million. How, between these two, he asked, can 120 million Japanese secure a future with a robust and improving standard of living? *Super Genba* answers Nishigaki's question.

After thirty-six years of advising some of Japan's biggest companies and twenty-four of these at the highest levels, I have had the most privileged access to Japanese top management of any foreigner in history. I have seen every problem imaginable and quite a few that I could not possibly have imagined.

People talk about Japan's lost generation. My view is that this loss could have easily been avoided with a few simple management changes. *Super Genba* is about those changes, the ten steps Japanese managers must take to bring Japan back to global leadership. These ten steps sum up my decades of recommendations in a management system that you can put to work immediately to get to the top in global markets.

Super Genba says that a business has a single function: to turn customer information into cash faster than its competition. Therefore, all business activities turn on only two processes:

- How much customer information you can build into your operation
- How fast you can turn that information into cash

Logically then, winning companies have, one, the largest customer interface or *genba* ("action+place") for inhaling customer information and, two, the processes to turn that information into cash fast. Managing these two well is the key to scaling profitably. Manage one or both badly and profitable scale is impossible to achieve.

What is not understood in Japan, however, is that as the cost of information falls you must inflate the *genba* to supersize. This is because it becomes ever cheaper and easier for companies to communicate with their customers in real time across an ever-wider front, and in ever more depth. As anyone who owns a smart phone knows, clouds accelerate this process to super speeds.

If your *genba* is not designed to inflate at these speeds, you lose.

A Super Genba is the combination of an expanding customer interface and high cash velocity, both driven by falling information costs. Super Genba control of the fast-expanding customer interface allows companies to appropriate the bulk of profits in their markets. *Genba* companies soak up all the losses.

Critically, turning customer information into cash is an ecosystem-wide process, not a product. This gives huge advantages to companies that are process-driven and that do not focus solely, or even at all, on products. The process by which companies interact with their customers in markets small and large, domestic and foreign, overwhelms all other things that they do. This customer interaction process, not products, is the primary generator of profit in all of today's markets.

Super Genba customer information and cash velocity processes are almost entirely absent in Japan's approach to foreign markets. The result is a crippling shrinkage in the only two dimensions that matter in business and the loss of market after market.

Japanese companies tend to focus on *monozukuri* ("thing+make"). This is as far removed from the super-sized, process-driven customer interface as it is possible to be. Many Japanese companies blindly pump more and more *monozukuri* products and versions of products into more and more markets—America and Europe yesterday; China, Brazil, and India today—on the assumption that something will succeed.

Layered onto a customer information void and low cash velocity operations, *monozukuri* is increasingly dilutive. By the time Kirk Nakamura, whom I was privileged to advise during his time as CEO of Panasonic, became CEO in 2000, the signs of trouble had been evident in Japanese industry for some time. Here's what he saw at Panasonic when he took over.

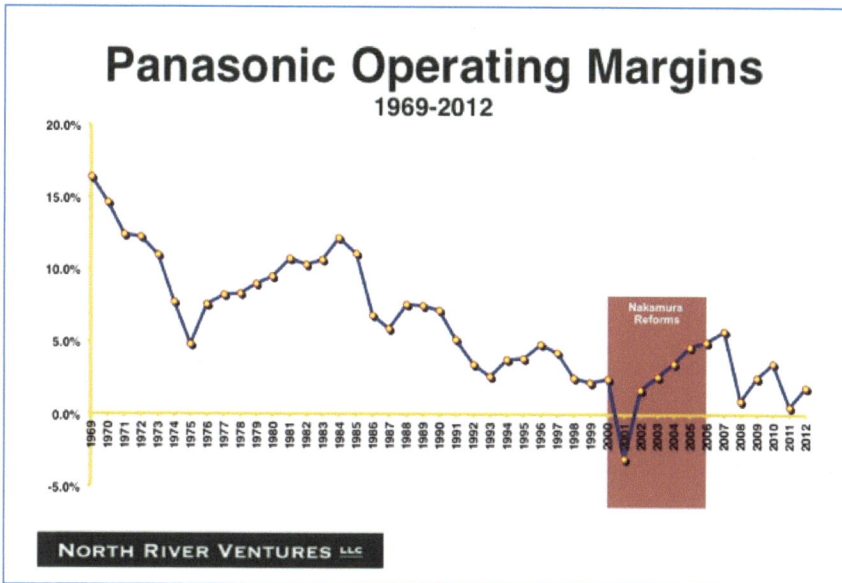

Panasonic Operating Margins
1969-2012

NORTH RIVER VENTURES LLC

Operating margins that were as high as 15-16% in the late 1960s when he was a young manager, had been falling for three decades with only periodic recoveries, like 1976-1984, but none to the 1969 high. It was a long period of decline from 1985 to 2001 that brought Kirk to the top job.

Some Panasonic managers thought that Panasonic's biggest problem was not operational. Rather, 1985 marked the impact of the Plaza Accords and the resulting rise of the yen—237 to the dollar then—to uncompetitive levels in the 110 to the dollar range. A few tweaks here and there and *voilà*! Panasonic would be back to its glory years.

Kirk knew that Panasonic's three-decade problem was more fundamental than the exchange rate. There must be core operational flaws and he sought in my Cash Velocity Management System (see Part One) a solution that would give him operational levers that would work deep into the company and could be used on a daily basis. I described in detail how he realigned the company to do this in my 2007 book, *Panasonic*.

The next step, as I described it in the last pages of *Panasonic*, was to be the "first-class demand management" that I now call Super Genba. Without this, I cautioned, the company "could find itself once again struggling to cut costs in a commodity business."[1] Sadly, this is exactly what happened, as the chart shows. Without Super Genba, profitable scale is elusive. Panasonic wound up with horrific losses. We will return to what happened at Panasonic and what can be done to turn the company around in the Conclusion.

In the middle of Koji Nishigaki's existential struggle, then, much of Japanese business finds itself completely mispositioned. The result is one lost generation and no way forward for the next.

Worse, the cost of not answering Nishigaki's question has gone way up since he posed Japan's dilemma over a decade ago and since Kirk started restructuring Panasonic. Japan is no longer a small United States with a domestic market big enough to build large companies that can treat foreign markets as incremental opportunities. In many ways, Japan has become another Canada, an incremental market that others can bypass at minimal loss while devoting their energies to major markets in the U.S., EU, and China. Being Canadian, I know that those in incremental markets like Japan face choices totally unlike those in major markets like the U.S. and China. Domestic demand is not enough. We must export or die. Japan's future depends almost entirely on how it adapts to foreign markets.

Japan must transform itself into a big Holland. It must be tightly integrated into its foreign markets to prosper. To grow, Japan must have a Super Genba.

Japan is well on the path to demographic collapse. So its integration into foreign markets is ever more critical for the country's long-term survival.

---

[1] Francis McInerney, *Panasonic,* St. Martins, 2007, p. 344

The solution is to enter high value markets by activating Super Genba processes immediately.

The great Japanese industrialist Konosuke Matsushita understood this well. He knew that market battles are won by combining control of the customer interface with cash velocity into a well-organized system. He was a relentless disintermediator, pushing ever closer to his customers and reorganizing his company whenever he saw a weakness in cash velocity. He knew that you win the market battle with *genba* organization first and your products second. The bigger your *genba*, the deeper customer information flows into your organization, the higher your cash velocity, and the more profitable your products will be. In my view, Konosuke's lessons have been forgotten.

I have sat through hundreds of meetings decade after decade where Japanese managers presented endless versions of products of all kinds—commercial, industrial, consumer—without a mention of foreign customers. No mention of a business model for selling these products either. And, what I find completely crazy, no one in these meetings ever seems to think this is unusual.

In late 2009, I sat through a week of presentations as group after group showed data where all their foreign markets, without exception, were falling year after year, and their share of those markets were falling still faster. But, because the Japanese markets for the same products were all rising and the company's market shares yet faster, these managers assumed that there must be something wrong with foreign customers or with their foreign sales staff. Or both. Group after group, no one in the room had any overseas experience and none could report on any ethnographic studies that might show the source of the problem and what the solution might be.

This problem was so endemic at Panasonic that Kirk wanted me to make my book *Panasonic* a textbook for the company showing how Konosuke would reform operations to get optimal cash velocity in the Internet age. And to show what the cost of not following the strictures of my cash velocity system would be. He had come to the top job older than most and knew that he would not be in office long enough to complete the job himself. It would take years more and he needed a text to guide the company long after his tenure.

Konosuke's great lesson was that, to turn customer information into cash quickly and effectively, you must know your customers personally. My inspiration is Hirostugu Morioka, the *taisho* of Michelin-starred Hirokawa in Osaka. *Taisho* knows his customers well and tailors everything to them, always showing new ways to think of classic sushi. Just like Konosuke with his products nearly a century ago. In *Super Genba* you will see how Konosuke would design an organization today that does this at cloud scale—the rate at which the cloud inflates—worldwide.

Japanese managers focus intensely on competitors, especially on those from other Asian countries like South Korea and China. They spend an inordinate amount of energy—expense—on competitor gazing. I always say, "Your competitors aren't paying you a single yen so why think about them at all?" As Konosuke taught, it's all about the customers. They pay. You deliver. Keep it simple and make money.

If you want to understand why there was a lost generation, my decades of meetings tell the story. With no customer information, there is nothing to turn into cash. The result is the parallel disaster of so many Japanese flagship companies.

When I go to Toronto, I like to drop into Asuka in Yorkville for sushi. When I greet *taisho* in my halting Japanese, he jokes that my French is definitely getting better. Last time, he gave me a lecture on how great Konosuke was. Then he just shook his head. "No one understands him in Japan today."

The *Super Genba* solution: Return to Konosuke, expand the *genba*, get the customer information, and put in place the IT and Big Data to turn this information into cash fast. This is the lesson Kirk and I wanted to spread seven years ago in *Panasonic* and it is ever more urgent today.

Inspired by Konosuke, *Super Genba* is a systematic solution to Japan's problems in foreign markets. *Super Genba* is a complete plan: You must take all of its ten steps all at once for the cure to be effective. Leave out even one part of the expanded *genba*, or even take the steps sequentially, and the rest will do little or nothing. Put all of *Super Genba* to work and you will see your global operations revived. Fail to put it to work and you have made a market exit decision.

In all the years I have worked with Japanese companies, I have only once seen an effective mechanism for communicating with overseas customers. Once. And it is a great story of smart management that shows that it can be done, and done well. It is the story of Nitto Denko and we will talk about this Super Genba example. What motivates Nitto is a simple fact of life: Sales in Japan that accounted for 70% of Nitto's total a decade ago account for only 28% today. Like it or not, Nitto had to see Japan as an incremental market, a large Holland, rather than as a small U.S. that can carry the company. This fact forced Super Genba changes in the company's thinking in everything from R&D to manufacturing and sales and from human resources to working capital management. In effect, everything that you will read in this book.

For the most part, however, no matter how well Japanese companies do at home, few in Japanese management know their overseas customers and still fewer understand how to add value for them consistently over the long term. This has to change. Quickly.

Japan's fast growing overseas customer information deficit cripples business decision-making. The wrong products reach the market at the wrong time or not at all. Customers are misidentified and not understood. Ethnography—the study of human behavior—is so poorly comprehended in Japan that I usually have to explain the word. Imagine companies churning out endless streams of products without ever doing a stroke of business or consumer ethnography. Crazy, right? But it happens every day.

I have on my desk large amounts of expensive product literature on energy systems that were translated directly from Japanese to English for the United States market. While the translation is excellent, the materials address only Japanese needs. The markets the product literature addresses either do not exist in the United States or function in ways that the product literature does not describe. In one case, a system with enough heft to run only my home is labeled as being suitable for a small cluster of homes which is absurd. Why spend so much money to show customers things they cannot use and how little you know about them?

I recently tried to build a global business that would have been worth about $40 billion to a Japanese company. I had identified the market myself. It was wholly new and had no competitors. The company had gone to great lengths to announce as strategic the technologies I planned to use. What I found was complete chaos at the customer interface, chaos that extended all the way back into the product development teams in Japan. This company had spent enormous sums on the products and systems I was trying to sell but had given no thought whatever to how to sell these. Indeed, it had not calculated the financial benefits to its customers of using its systems. Worse, it did not know how to do this so it could not have calculated these benefits even if it wanted to.

A couple of years ago, the same company showed me a large array of related industrial products from several of its divisions that cost billions to develop. Yet it occurred to no one that, if attached on a cloud server, these products would become a powerful engine of cash for customers worldwide.

The company thought it was selling technologies that customers would buy because ... well, no one could tell me.

Later, when I identified a global customer that could use just such a cloud-based system to generate large amounts of cash, the company replied that it could not sell globally to a single customer, only to the customer's local operations one country at a time. And that each country operation made its own decisions about cloud systems and some had none at all. And not all products were available in all markets. To buy from this Japanese company, the customer's U.S.-based global Chief Information Officer would have to meet with dozens of teams from around the world, each with its own agenda and capabilities. He was expected to mix and match these himself and bring in competitors to fill the inevitable gaps country-by-country. How this makes sense is beyond me. It is throwing billions of dollars off the Tokyo Sky Tree.

Japanese managers often talk of what they call the Galapagos Syndrome, the idea that Japanese customers evolve in isolation from world markets and therefore Japanese products are maladapted to foreign customers. Those same managers then do nothing to get out there and work with their overseas customers to create products and services that do sell and create the financial models to show customers how they can benefit.

This is not complicated. If your products don't sell, move to your customers, study them closely—indeed personally, as Konosuke did—and create products and services that do sell profitably. Stay-at-home management doesn't work. Put the Super into the *genba.* Push the whole company into the *genba.*

Super Genba is about designing company-wide *genba* processes that generate customer information premiums, the kind of information surfeit that builds profitable long-term relationships that you can tap for decades, not just for single product cycles.

Do this right and, as A.G. Lafley, the CEO of Proctor and Gamble who spent many years in Japan, says, "The orders will write themselves."

The crying shame is that the Chinese government insists as a matter of policy that Chinese companies not use the kinds of IT, Big Data, and cloud systems essential to a Super Genba structure.[2] For *raisons d'état*, China will compete only in the lowest possible value end of every market, ceding to others all the high-value, cloud-dominated markets of the future. Japan can have all the best customers and markets it chooses. But it must use *Super Genba* to get them.

If Japan continues to compete head-to-head with China using low-value *genba* customer interfaces, it will be crushed.

Another IT value is that, as Sean White and I showed nearly twenty years ago in *The Total Quality Corporation* (Dutton, 1995), by substituting clean and cheap information for other resources like land, labor, and capital, first class IT fosters lower costs and higher quality than dirty alternatives. You only have to spend a few minutes in China to realize that the country is polluting itself to death. I regard my visits to China as dangerous to my health; the shorter they are, the better. This can only mean that China's production systems are Neanderthal and doomed to a similar evolutionary end.

The *Super Genba* lesson, therefore, is that Information Technology is not a cost to be reduced, as so many Japanese managers think. IT is a Super Genba cash accelerator and customer information engine to be maximized. For example, each day of sales at Panasonic is $219 million and a week is $1.5 billion—a lot of money. Getting Panasonic's days of sales in inventory and receivables to where Apple is today would free up a staggering $12.5 billion on its balance sheet. Put another way, if Apple operated like Panasonic, it would

[2] Mozur, Paul. "China's 'Wall' Hits Business." *AllThingsD*. February 15, 2013. http://allthingsd.com/20130214/chinas-wall-hits-business/

carry an additional $25 billion on its balance sheet. But, if it was that heavily loaded up it could not have scaled so profitably and surpassed its Japanese competitors so easily.

The only question management needs to ask is, how much will we spend to accelerate the conversion of customer information into cash? I know of few Japanese companies that think this way today. The result is the lost generation.

An excuse I often get in Japan is that cash velocity is low because that's just the way it is in whatever market a company is targeting. Well, it isn't and anyone who knows how modern markets work knows this. We will see in *Super Genba* Step Two how Nitto Denko cut receivables in one industrial market from 140 days to 15 simply by changing a process. No new products, no special technology. Just a process. And, in changing that process, it put itself in a position to gain customer information in real time that no competitor sees. From this it was able to accelerate sales, launch products ahead of the competition, and do this extremely profitably. You can do the same thing. But you have to know your customers intimately to do it.

Because it is about turning customer information into cash, *Super Genba* is about managing the velocity of cash across a company's eco system, which includes its suppliers, customers, and itself. Modern companies are designed primarily to optimize their cash velocities (Apple, Walmart, and Proctor and Gamble are good examples), not primarily to control costs, something that is poorly understood in Japan.

The simplest way to understand the success of Walmart is that it is a cluster of stores hung off a customer information-to-cash acceleration engine. Apple is a set of cloud access devices like iPhones arrayed on a cloud to do the same thing. Markets everywhere are breaking into dyads with Super Genba top predators like Walmart and Apple on one side and clusters of poor performing *genba* prey like Sharp on the other.

Super Genba says that no top line initiative, no matter how well planned, can succeed if cash velocity is low.

One of the biggest mistakes in Japanese business is breaking this rule, as Sharp did with its giant Sakai LCD operations. Sharp put the cart before the horse. Sakai was dropped into a bloated supply chain and failing sales operation, both of which were easily evident when Sakai was planned from Sharp's 51 days of sales in inventory and 82 days in receivables. Sharp soon ran into trouble. If it took me a few seconds to see this, what was management thinking about? It wasn't thinking, obviously. We will devote more to this in Part One.

Some Japanese companies go backward. Panasonic, which was progressing nicely with my system under CEO Kirk Nakamura, stopped using the system when he retired, built the huge plasma TV factory at Amagasaki, an equally imposing LCD factory at Himeji, and fell straight off a cliff.

Super Genba is about adapting to the post *monozukuri* world in which everything is appified on the cloud so that products, processes, communications, and apps run together in a single flow that I call Hyper Monozukuri. This Hyper Monozukuri space now dominates markets. Those who understand Hyper Monozukuri, as Apple and Nitto do, expand their *genba* into the new, fast-inflating space and take ever-bigger shares of global markets. Those who don't, like Hewlett-Packard, Nokia, and Panasonic, are being sidelined. Many of the sidelined will never recover. *Super Genba* is about making sure that you are not one of these.

Super Genba-designed companies allow customers to set company priorities, Konosuke-style. I see far too many Japanese companies that operate on internal priorities, wasting colossal amounts of time on unproductive activities and decisions that are *a propos* of nothing. One of my favorites is shuffling divisions and cutting costs without reforming cash velocity and restructuring the customer interface. Predictably, as at Panasonic, the old system, unchanged, resurfaces after a short time, stunning management that thought it had made all the changes needed.

Super Genba is about time. I cannot tell you how many Japanese managers complain to me that world markets are moving too fast for their decision cycles. By the time they make a decision, markets have already moved, and their decisions are out of date.

There is a reason for this: Traditional Japanese *genba* structures are not designed for customer information flows big and fast enough for modern decision-making in real time. In many cases, Japanese companies make decisions that better customer-informed foreign companies bypass by outsourcing or pushing these onto cloud operations in order to reduce time-to-cash. The result is way too much time making decisions that have no value for customers and so lengthen time-to-cash. In a *Super Genba* organization, the customer weighs so heavily on the company that it squeezes out these time lapses and accelerates cash velocity.

The lack of IT optimized for Super Genba processes slows the inflow of customer information to a crawl and with it the speed of decision-making and cash velocity. You see this in the slow uptake of Cisco-style telepresence teleconferencing systems, even though Japan invented high definition television. Managers are forever traveling across the globe when they could be meeting on Skype. Travel costs are horrendous, not to mention the waste in time. I've even had problems sending common email attachments to Japanese companies because their servers are designed only for small files. What possible purpose can this serve except to diminish customer relations and cripple demand management?

In an example of how system-wide slowdowns can hurt, in early 2013, I reviewed a semiconductor operation that was in trouble. The team sent in to fix the problem had forests worth of paper crammed with charts and graphs only a handful of which were useful. Like every Canadian, I know that you can't make decisions about which way to drive in the middle of a blizzard. This team was frozen in a blizzard of useless information while valuable time rushed by.

I pointed to the salient data, showed the team that it had choices, and gave it an aggressive timeline with project completion in nine months and a return to profitability in twelve. The team recognized that it could not make so many big decisions that fast and instead exited the market. This, even though its products could have revolutionized the fast inflating world of cloud computing, turning the division into a global powerhouse in a very short time. Put another way, when offered the chance to grow sales and profits at cloud scale, time was such a problem that the team could not move.

This issue of time at cloud scale presents new problems to business. Nearly twenty years ago I came up with the concept of Moore Time, or time as information costs fall along the Moore Curve proposed by Intel cofounder Gordon Moore in 1965.

The idea is simple. There is normal time in minutes, hours, and days, and there is time on the Moore Curve where the cost of information drops fast. Is there a difference, I asked myself in 1995, between an organization that operates in normal time and one that is optimized to work in Moore Time on the falling Information Cost Curve?[3]

The answer is, yes. You can easily explain the difference between Apple and its competitors this way. And we will see how in *Super Genba* Part One.

The advent of cloud computing, a logical extension of the Moore Curve to the point where every business, person, and thing has access to unlimited computing at marginal cost—basically zero—accentuates the problem.

---

[3] *Black Holes and Dematerialization*, North River Ventures LLC, October 1995

Here is how this works. Because the cloud is a function of the Moore Curve, it inflates as a function of three things, all moving exponentially: the number of cloud connected processors times the power of these processors on the Moore Curve times the power of apps they support. Each of these fast-moving vectors inflates the cloud into our Zetabyte Era and, therefore, inflates the Super Genba space.

The Big Data on customers that you get from your cloud-inflated Super Genba is determinative. If your *genba* does not expand at cloud scale with Cloud Inflation, you have no Big Data, nothing on which to act and add value, and you vanish. Seen in this light, cloudless Panasonic's troubles make complete sense. As do the troubles of Sony, Sharp, and others.

Super Genba is about ensuring that you operate at cloud scale in Moore Time, that your *genba* expands at the rate at which information costs fall, and that you make fast, effective decisions.

As falling information costs expand the *genba*, they progressively disintermediate markets. If your company is designed for the costly, multilayered-distribution structure of the 1950s, your *genba* is tiny, you have missed half a century of Moore Curve-driven disintermediation cycles, and you have a lot of catching up to do.

A painful example is the consumer electronics sector. Japanese consumer electronics companies rely on long-obsolete retail intermediaries overseas, like Best Buy in the U.S., that get sales of hundreds of dollars per square foot. In Best Buy's case, $823. Apple, which sells directly to its customers, gets $5,647, or nearly seven times Best Buy's sales per square foot. Apple is now the most successful retail operation since Mitsui invented the department store in the early 17ᵗʰ century. Japanese CE companies are, instead, relying on the weakest link to their markets. Many of these intermediaries are in trouble. Circuit City went under in

18

2008, as I predicted it would in 2007,[4] and troubled Best Buy is closing stores and trying to recapitalize itself. Relying on these distributors in the cloud age would have driven Konosuke absolutely mad. *Super Genba* is about putting an end to this and ensuring that Japanese companies sell one way to their customers and one way only: directly.

Super Genba is about brand. Your brand is how you manage your customers' experience of your products and services. Logic says that whomever has the largest *genba* has the largest brand envelope, and therefore the most market control. Putting the Super in the *genba* is how you get a world-beating brand envelope in which to manage customers.

Super Genba is about making M&A accretive. The number one reason that so many deals fail to generate value is that most are mergers between low cash velocity companies with limited Super Genba potential. You see this every day, and the collapse of these deals is easy to predict. I just look at the cash velocities of the merging companies. If either party's cash velocity is low, I know that the deal is dead before it is signed. This never fails.

A great example that we will discuss in detail in *Super Genba* Step Nine was Compaq's acquisition of DEC. In February 1998, I wrote that buying DEC would derail Compaq because DEC's cash velocity was in a stall. Expect a value meltdown, I said.[5] In April 1999, investors got exactly that. Compaq shares went through the floor and the CEO and CFO were fired. By September 2001, Compaq was on the block. Hewlett-Packard made the mistake of buying Compaq and never recovered. One cash velocity miscalculation and the damage continues fifteen years later. This is a mistake no one can afford to make.

---

[4] *Retail Revolution,* North River Ventures LLC, May 8, 2007

[5] *Breaking the Moore Time Barrier,* North River Ventures LLC, February 1998, p. 2

How about when the private equity group comprising of Sumitomo Mitsui Banking Corp., Daiwa Securities SMBC Co., and lead by Goldman Sachs, got in trouble after buying about ¥300 billion in preferred stock in low cash velocity Sanyo in 2006? The preferred stock translated into 70% of the company and a valuation of ¥1 trillion.

Due diligence on Sanyo's cash velocity should have told the Goldman group that it had to replace the whole management team with expert outsiders and rebuild all of the company's IT systems, supply chains, and sales operations globally. This in turn would have lead Goldman to ask the obvious question: Do we have the management bench to oversee this process?

Evidently unaware of any of the pitfalls, the Goldman team went ahead, got poor results, and when the market collapsed in late 2008, found that no one would take it out at the amount needed to make it whole.[6]

Seeing this, I wrote in December 2008 that because of its low cash velocity, Sanyo could not possibly be accretive for any buyer.[7] Panasonic stepped in to buy the company regardless for a reported ¥806.7 billion. Goldman took a 20% bath. In the next five years Panasonic lost $20 billion.

Simple cash velocity due diligence would have obviated all these problems.

Just as low cash velocities reveal problems, high velocities confer enormous advantages. Because high cash velocities result in lower working capital loads and higher Operating Free Cash Flow (OFCF) for the same sales volumes, high velocity companies have the advantages of scalable profitability that others don't have.

---

[6] "Goldman Ends Talks to Sell Stake in Sanyo to Panasonic" *The Wall Street Journal*, November 27, 2008.

[7] *Private Equity Failure in Parallel*, North River Ventures LLC, December 2, 2008.

Super Genba is about allocating human resources optimally. If your *genba* is too small, you don't have enough customer information to tell you how to allocate your most valuable resource, your people. If your *genba* is big enough, management gets enough customer information to tell it who should be put where and how many of these should be men or women, Japanese or non-Japanese, and life-long employees or new hires with well established outside expertise, and where they should be located.

Simple math says that as your *genba* expands with Cloud Inflation, you cannot possibly fill it with life-long employees who have no experience with the cloud. Putting the super into the *genba* means a radical shift in hiring, training, and promotion strategies.

You can see that the *genba* of Japanese companies is not as big as the market needs because while women are 50% of all consumer and business customers worldwide, you almost never meet women in positions of authority in Japan. This says that Japanese companies have not adapted to the number of female customers. Thus, Japanese companies look nothing like their customers, something that makes selling to them incomparably more difficult than it needs to be.

In addition, failure to use the powerful female mind to solve complex problems explains why even after inventing cell phone apps, Japan could not come up with a world-dominating iPhone. This is not hard to figure out. Men and women think differently and approach problem solving differently, so adding a woman to a solid base of men does not add one more employee arithmetically along a single axis. Rather, it adds a second axis, and expands problem-solving abilities in multiple dimensions. You can see very quickly who will win this battle. Male monocultures will lose every time.

A Japanese supplier to Apple told me of its discomfiture being in a room with so many women decision makers and having none on its own side of the table. This is not a formula for a good long-term relationship.

Japan's lack of women managers therefore magnifies the risks of product and service failure to unacceptable levels. Activating women is not about managing diversity; it is about reducing risks and building profits.

The Economist records Japan as ranking twenty-fifth in the world in its use of the educated female labor force, far behind economic jokes like Greece.[8] This huge pool of untapped expertise is a major disability, especially during a demographic implosion. But, if Japan can mobilize its reserve army of educated women fast, it has a chance at Super Genba success.

Mobilizing the reserve army of women slowly or not at all has frightening implications. Ginni Rometty, who runs IBM, broke through all the major barriers that kept her out of contention for the top job thirty years ago. If Japan starts now and moves forward at the same rate as the United States, it will not be globally competitive until 2043. But, by then Japan will be a Chinese fiefdom.

Want to beat China? Use *Super Genba* to build market power by putting more of your best people in front of more of your best customers more of the time. Get the human resources calculation right with the mix of men and women that moves the right people into the fast inflating *genba* at the right time. Mobilize Japan's reserve army of women, fast.

The same can be said for the mix of Japanese and non-Japanese in top management. Many years ago an American working for a Japanese company told me that, "we all know that we could never survive at GE." In other words, "because our performance will never give us a shot at the top job in our Japanese company, real performers go where they can compete for executive rank. We are the leftovers."

---

[8] "The Glass-ceiling Index." *The Economist*, March 7, 2013.

This company got the results it was planning for. Sales stagnated in the U.S. year after year. Profits evaporated, and no number of management changes or new products and technologies had any impact.

One of the smartest moves Nitto Denko made was to integrate Japanese and non-Japanese in its all-English language corporate education system for top managers. CEO Yukio Nagira personally assigns them the toughest problems that the company has. Both he and past CEO Masamichi Takemoto spend days with these teams as they work through the issues. The manager of Nitto's corporate education operation, Tsune Katsura, is a seasoned line manager with global experience rather than a longtime member of HQ staff. This combination of leaders brings a measure of reality to the process that others often miss.

By the end of the Nitto process, managers have learned to work as a team across cultural and language barriers, and the company leadership has a firm idea of who can do top jobs, who cannot, and where the next executives will come from. The results include some of the best global market attack plans I have seen in my four decades in business. And a selection of upcoming non-Japanese managers from which a CEO could eventually be chosen. Anyone can do this. It costs nothing and reduces costs and risks. But few do.

As an organization tool, *Super Genba* can help overcome the limitations of the Japanese language. The first thing you learn when you study Japanese is that, unlike English (or French, which I also speak), no one is inventing new *kanji*. The *kanji* for "car" contains a horse-drawn cart as it was used thousands of years ago. Part of the *kanji* in "to study" is a woman delivering a baby, signifying "struggle." Both are graphic and clear but, like most *kanji*, of no use in describing modern business processes that change every day and that need a new language to describe them.

There is the buffer script of *katagana*, which is a sort of storeroom for foreign words, but this too has limitations. In English we write foreign words more or less as they sound to foreigners and as they spell them if they use an alphabet. Japanese instead renders foreign words into the 104 sounds of the Japanese language written in *katagana*. In a Japanese language class I took years ago, an American student complained to our teacher about learning 4,000 *kanji*. She complained right back about having to learn 10,000 English vowel sounds. Pushing those 10,000, forget about the consonants, into only 104 renders foreign words meaningless to Japanese and non-Japanese alike. Take the simple *katagana* for television. It is spoken *terebi*, which sounds nothing like television or even TV and is not recognizable to an English speaker. So, *katagana* keeps hidden from Japanese the real meaning of foreign words and keeps hidden from non-Japanese what the Japanese mean by using *katagana*. Sometimes the Japanese have distinct meanings for *katagana* words that are only tangentially related to the foreign words from which they were derived. *Katagana* is not at all helpful.

Also, there is a time element to *katagana*. A word newly created in English to describe an advanced business process might take a decade to make it into its *katagana* form, by which time it may be obsolete. When it does make it into *katagana*, it is not clear that it is understood in Japan as it is in the original. To make the case, I am inventing a word for this book, the Apposphere for the ever- expanding swirl of cloud-based apps. We shall see how long it takes to enter the common *katagana* lexicon and be understood there the way I intend it.

This language problem may sound like a minor nuisance. It isn't. Take something that businesses must do every day, educate their customers. This is a continuous process that successful companies like Apple and Walmart do religiously. In the Japanese language, however, you cannot say "customer education" because the customer, *o kyaku sama*, or

Great Lord Customer, educates you, not the other way around. Thus, even though language scholars like Guy Deutscher and John McWhorter say this is impossible and that all languages can say the same thing, "customer education" is a file that simply does not exist in Japanese. But without it, you cannot sell anything in the modern world.

Translation: While their competitors have been educating customers across a fast-inflating customer interface for decades and taking all the profitable sales, Japanese companies have been left with the unprofitable remains. You probably cannot estimate the amount of foregone revenue and profits attributable to the lack of only two words, "customer education." To solve this, *Super Genba* is a complete system in which customer education is inherent in the process, obviating the need for words that you may not feel comfortable using.

In another example, for years I used the phrase "global account management" which in English means the full set of *Super Genba* operations required to manage and, notably, educate large customers across their operations worldwide. My team of translators long rendered it as "financial management," something to which it is unrelated, and I could not understand why no one got what I meant. This lack of linguistic transparency probably cost the company where I first used the phrase a good $50 billion a year in foregone sales overseas. All its top line initiatives went straight into a void.

To get past this problem I take three Japanese words, starting, of course with *genba*, and adding *monozukuri* and *kizuna* and use them in a way that I have tested out for some time on clients and in the LinkedIn discussion group, Business In Japan. *Super Genba*, the title of this book, is the name I put to the process of managing a modern business. Hyper Monozukuri is appified *monozukuri* in a cloud apposphere. And *kizuna*, inspired by the *taisho* of a great sushi bar in Osaka's Kyobashi district who named his place *kizuna*, is the result your business should get, a family-like and highly profitable bond with your best customers worldwide. I think the ever-imaginative Konosuke would approve of my approach.

Super Genba uses these three words. I will tie everything to them so that Japanese managers can understand in the simplest, clearest way possible what I mean.

Super Genba is about setting customer-based priorities, not internally generated ones, and discarding everything that does not meet customer priorities and those alone. This means having an intimate understanding of customers and having the systems and methods to turn their priorities into actions quickly and effectively. Not doing this means having large numbers of enormously talented people wasting time on activities that have no place in customer thinking.

Super Genba is about doubling your sales profitably like a McDonald's or an Apple. It means managing the rate of Cloud Inflation in our Zetabyte world. Cloud computing inflates just like the early universe, reshaping everything as it does so, and I will explain how this impacts your business in the following chapters. Let me say here simply that, to scale profitably, your organization must be designed to act in a coordinated fashion right across the fast-inflating Zetabyte universe. You must think and act at cloud scale.

My sister-in-law, Sandy Raskopf, a logistics genius, keeps McDonald's operations in North America down to one day of sales in inventory. Every extra day is about $75 million on McDonald's balance sheet; a week is more than half a billion dollars. Keeping McDonald's this trim is key to how it more than doubled operating profit on sales increase of 32% over the 2004-2011 period. How does she do it? The right IT and a lot of attention to the details that the IT throws up.

If you want a really dramatic example, voters returned Barak Obama to the U.S. presidency in 2012 because his campaign *genba* scaled to super size with the cloud. His competitor, Mitt Romney, did not use cloud-based IT and did not reach the voters essential to winning. As a result, he and his team knew much less about voters or what they expected in a President. In a sense, he moved away from voters at the rate of Cloud Inflation. He never addressed the voters that his limited *genba* could not see. He proposed only policies that interested voters in his small *genba*, and he lost.[9]

Similarly, Japanese companies think they can win customers from which they are moving away at the rate of Cloud Inflation. It does not work because it cannot work. You cannot sell to those you cannot see. As physicist Roger Penrose would say, they are outside your light cone.

In the Zetabyte Era, the cloud is the *genba*. It is the Big Data space where you interact with your customers wherever they are in the world in real time. Every Apple computer calls home—back to Apple's iCloud servers—between 2:00 a.m. and 4:00 a.m. local time, so that Apple can update everything it needs to know for its products to work for you. It even adjusts for time zones when you travel. Every time you touch your iPhone or iPad, you touch Apple's iCloud servers. These help Apple amass unprecedented Big Data on its customers. That is a hugely expanded *genba*. If Apple's cloud-based *genba* works for your customers better than yours does, you lose. If Konosuke were alive today, he would talk endlessly about using the cloud to get to customers. And he would act at cloud speed.

I am always amazed by how little of what companies like Apple do is understood in Japan. I remember decoding Apple almost a decade ago for one of Japan's biggest brands,

---

[9] Rutenberg, Jim. "The Obama Campaign's Digital Masterminds Cash In." *The New York Times*, June 20, 2013, sec. Magazine. See also: Draper, Robert. "Can the Republicans Be Saved From Obsolescence?" *The New York Times*, February 14, 2013, sec. Magazine

explaining in detail how Apple would attack, take all their premium customers, and with them all the profit, in several sectors simultaneously. From this, I created a powerful set of strategies to counter Apple's fast-inflating *genba* and take all the profits before Apple could.

I was told in response that since none of this was *monozukuri*, it could not be contemplated. Instead, "Show us McInerney-san, how this will work for a *monozukuri* company." The idea that simple *monozukuri* could not work on first principles was not thinkable. All those profits and markets were lost just as I knew very well ten years ago that they would be. Disaster followed. This once famous brand is no longer a player in global consumer electronics.

The all-important message of *Super Genba* is that it can be done. Nitto Denko used the Super Genba system to gain rapid growth and double digit operating income on one of its key divisions, powering its stock to nearly twice the growth of the S&P 500 since the depth of the Great Recession in December 2008. And seventeen times the Nikkei. Nitto trades at a healthy 1.7 times sales.

What makes Nitto such a performer? First, a set of three successive CEOs—Hideki Yamamoto, Masamichi Takemoto, and Yukio Nagira—who, over a long period of time, relentlessly questioned their own assumptions about every aspect of Nitto's global markets and about how Nitto polymers could be used to create large, high-value market niches. Second, a huge amount of hard work by a lot of people to put in place better and better answers to these questions year after year. Nitto did not become a top performer overnight. It took the consistent effort of thousands of managers and employees at all levels, functions, and geographies to make this a reality.

When the test came in the Great Recession, Nitto bounced back at speed, proving to itself that its new system is resilient and that change must continue in order to keep the answers to its core questions coming. The company took careful stock of how it did this, reflecting in an internal paper for top managers on what went right and what went wrong.

In an example of sheer brilliance that I mentioned earlier, Nitto invented a process to add to core products that cut its receivable days by a staggering 90%, significantly accelerating its own cash velocity and that of its customers, lowering balance sheet risks for both. All at no cost in R&D and with a huge improvement in SG&A efficiency. Super Genba at its best.

There is more to this picture. Nitto replaced all of its top managers, rebuilt its global sales organization, its R&D and manufacturing operations, most in-country operations, its working capital management, capital expenditure planning, organization structure, and corporate education. In other words, everything.

This is how real change is made. Think through customer needs and the processes required to turn customer information into cash fast in your entire ecosystem so that you and your customers both get material cash velocity benefits from using your products. Then apply what you have learned with care, diligence, and lots of *kaizen*.

You can use *Super Genba* to become a winner. But you have to be prepared to do what it takes. You have to recognize fear on the faces of your managers. I have seen this in the form of anger, bluster, disdain, contempt, outright rejection, no reaction at all, and my favorite, a smile. In every case it boils down to naked fear. You must also accept that not all managers are created equally and many will not make the grade. In *Super Genba*, no one can hide. Everyone in the company feels the remorseless heat from customers all the time and many employees will get burned. You have to be ready for this.

Super Genba follows a simple logic. In Part One, we will look at the core problem that is reshaping business models the world over, the falling cost of information. Next, you will grade your company using my simple system. This grade will tell you if you can scale profitably or not during an era of fast-falling information costs. Then, in Part Two, we will look the ten steps you must take to put *Super Genba* to work for your company:

1. Super Genba Step One: Use the Cloud

2. Super Genba Step Two: Drive Sales

3. Super Genba Step Three: Manage Innovation

4. Super Genba Step Four: Manage Manufacturing

5. Super Genba Step Five: Build a Superior Brand

6. Super Genba Step Six: Manage Human Resources

7. Super Genba Step Seven: Design Your Organization

8. Super Genba Step Eight: Manage Your IT

9. Super Genba Step Nine: Manage Mergers and Acquisitions

10. Super Genba Step Ten: Manage Customer Service

Who should read *Super Genba?* Managers at every level and in every function in every Japanese company. *Super Genba* is about entire organizations. Whether you are in a front line setting like sales or manufacturing or in a secondary setting like human resources or financial management, *Super Genba* includes you. It leaves no part of the organization untouched from the CEO to an R&D project manager or a field sales rep. This all inclusiveness is the "super" in the *genba*.

PART ONE: UNDERSTANDING THE WORLD OF INFORMATION

The Problem: Getting Ahead of the Information Cost Curve

The idea behind *Super Genba* began a long time ago. In 1967 when we were teenagers in high school, the Canadian author Michael Barnholden, who now teaches at the Emily Carr University in Vancouver, told me to read Marshall McLuhan's new book *Understanding Media*. "This," he said, "is cool, man."

Understanding Media was the second volume in a two-part series. The first, *The Gutenberg Galaxy*, was published in 1962 by the University of Toronto.

McLuhan's central idea was simple: Take a message, say the daily news, send it over various kinds of media from word-of-mouth to newspaper to TV, and the impact of the medium will change the message itself. So: same story, change the medium, and you get a different story. Whence McLuhan's famous dictum: "The medium is the message."

What McLuhan proposed was that new media technologies don't just change how we do things but what we do. New media like the cloud don't just change how the *genba* works but what it does.

We see McLuhan's information alchemy every day when a director turns a top-selling book into a movie. No matter how "true" to the book, the impact of the big screen changes the story, often making it unrecognizable. Clouds do the same thing.

McLuhan went farther, saying that, as the medium changes, how you use it would change you too. You change the tool and the tool changes you. Change the *genba* and the *genba* changes you. How this works is what *Super Genba* is about.

McLuhan's prime example was the bloody and tumultuous European Reformation. When movable type transformed the Bible from hard-to-find handwritten manuscripts copied laboriously over decades to cheaply printed and reprinted books that could be shipped anywhere, the power structure of society shifted entirely. With cheap printing, the means of information production dispersed quickly to those who had not previously had any economic or political power. The Europe of the Treaty of Westphalia looked nothing like the Europe of Henry Tudor just over a century earlier. As with clouds today, human behavior changed in enormously disruptive ways that no one anticipated and none could manage.

For the first time since Gutenberg's 1440 press we have something incomparably more disruptive: the cloud, which grants ubiquitous access by every business, person, and thing to unlimited computing at marginal cost, or zero. Just as the inexpensive press accelerated the number of published books from thousands kept from public view in monasteries to millions in people's homes in a few decades, in our Cloud Age data is so cheap that its rate of dispersion on every device imaginable is an explosive force. Data volumes have inflated from megabytes to zetabytes in less than twenty years.

This is the age of cloud-born Big Data. Human behavior is once again changing in disruptive ways we did not anticipate and know little about how to manage. Those who have a *genba* super-sized enough to profit from these disruptions will win. Those who do not will lose.

McLuhan also said that organizations from different media eras—like the clouded and unclouded we see now—coexist.

> An age in rapid transformation is one which exists on the frontier between two cultures and between conflicting technologies. Every moment of (the age) is an act of translation of each of these cultures into the other. Today we live on the frontier between five centuries of mechanism and the new electronics, between

the homogeneous and the simultaneous. It is painful but fruitful.[10]

Joseph Schumpeter's "creative destruction" occurs all along McLuhan's frontier. When Kirk Nakamura was CEO of Panasonic, he never tired of warning of this shift in the tectonic plates of business.

As in our Cloud Age, for quite some time after the Reformation began, large *genba* print-age organizations and small *genba* manuscript-age organizations existed side by side, staring at each other across a great ideological divide, and fighting each other ferociously in war after war without really understanding each other's premises.

McLuhan's observations about shifting behavior are crucial in understanding the *genba-Super* Genba divide: CEOs operating in the pre-cloud *genba* era cannot see the same choices as competitor CEOs in the same market who operate in the Super Genba cloud era. If your *genba* is too small to see your market, you can't make decisions about it. The result is a set of management behaviors that are not only mutually incompatible but also mutually incomprehensible. *Super Genba* is about making sure you can see your customers well enough that you can create the future rather than be run over by it.

In the cloud era information costs fall along the Moore Curve—a world where, as Intel co-founder Gordon Moore predicted, computer processor price-performance doubles every eighteen months. In this fast-shifting world, the *genba*-Super Genba divide among companies isn't jarring; it's horrifying. We are talking about a lot of lost jobs and value meltdowns in very short periods.

This is why, for example, a well-trained CEO like Carly Fiorina, who was sacked by Hewlett-Packard, can make

---

[10] McLuhan, Marshall, *The Gutenberg Galaxy*, University of Toronto Press, 1962, p. 141.

decisions so unlike those of Steve Jobs, even though they were in the same industry. These managers lived in *genba* worlds of different dimensions and different decision matrices. Yet they competed against each other for the same customers. This is what happened to Blackberry and Nokia.

Intuitively, it is not hard to see who will come out on top in the *genba*-Super Genba divide. But intuition won't do. We must give management data on which to bridge the divide, so CEOs can understand the dimensions of the universe of their customers and what they have to do to take out-sized, profitable market share.

I've spent decades trying to help business leaders in Japan, Canada, the United States, and Europe understand the impact of McLuhan's IT-driven *genba*-Super Genba frontier on their decision making. The number of CEOs who get this is tiny. At Google, Apple, and Amazon, they certainly do. It is not easy. Hence the need for a complete Super Genba system.

In 1967, I realized that each of McLuhan's media ages co-terminated with major shifts in organization design in everything from states to religions and, of course, companies. So, change the media and you change organizations. On this point McLuhan and I owe much to Harold Innis who taught economics at the University of Toronto, knew McLuhan, and greatly influenced him. McLuhan wrote that both *The Gutenberg Galaxy* and *Understanding Media* were footnotes to Innis' 1950 book *Empire and Communications*, making *Super Genba* a footnote to a couple of footnotes.

Innis wrote that different empires (we can read businesses) from the Egyptian to the British were held together by different communications technologies. The efficiency of each communication technology determined the empire's geography and longevity.

Papyrus, he said, enabled one kind of empire, Egypt, and paper enabled another, Islam. Communications technologies, he said, alter our use of space and time and so dictate the structure of our organizations, whatever they are. Most CEOs see what Innis meant every day. Like the difference between *genba* and Super Genba, print supports only hierarchical organizations with small exposure to customers, while the cloud enables flat and virtual organizations with almost unlimited exposure to customers.

While Innis and McLuhan were intellectually stimulating, the question I had was how to make their ideas practical. I saw in 1967 that each of their media ages could better be understood as acceleration in the speed of information across organizations. Movable type is faster than handwritten manuscripts or word of mouth, and electronic media are infinitely faster again. I simplified their thinking into a single sentence: The velocity of information is always increasing.

In July 1968, I got a chance to test my theory and created the first Super Genba prototype. The Toronto Board of Education launched a summer experiment in free-form education called SEED for Shared Exploration, Experience, and Discovery. SEED was a response to the Government of Ontario's Hall-Dennis Report of the previous year that had been highly critical of traditional Ontario education. Being something of a student radical, I had started an underground, or unofficial, newspaper in my high school that was much more critical than Hall-Dennis. I went down to SEED to interview the people there to prove to my readers that they had no idea of what they were doing. I was going to publish a damning story.

What I found was struggling, on the verge of collapse. But I also found a superior leader, Les Birmingham, who is to this day my model CEO. He admitted openly that neither he nor his small staff, all long-time education professionals from the old system, had the expertise to make a free form school operational. But his goal intrigued me and I offered to pull SEED together using my information velocity theory. To my astonishment, Les said yes and put all his weight behind my efforts. Like all great CEOs, he knew when to let people get on with the job and allowed our team to set our own benchmarks for success.

My idea at SEED was to accelerate the velocity of information in education by building a school on a phone, the only network of the day, rather than on a traditional building. McLuhan had talked of the coming world of "electric-all-at-onceness" (the Internet was only invented in 1968 and did not become popularized for another thirty years) in which there was no up, no down, no near, and no far. Everything would exist in an immediately accessible electronic space.

Decades before Amazon.com, McLuhan predicted what became one of the biggest *genba*-to-Super Genba transformations in business: You will not go to the library, it will come to you.

I thought the phone would do this for us. With everything on a network, such as it was, we could move resources to students in real time rather than students to resources in school time. A fundamental *genba*-to-Super Genba process innovation that I hoped would advance results well beyond anything then available in bricks and mortar institutions. This would be the first major change in education since classrooms emerged at the end of the Dark Ages.

In my theory, education at higher information velocities would change not just how people learned, but what they learned. Which is what happened. We pioneered the teaching of particle physics to high school students and had them writing code for large IBM mainframe computers years before the Toronto Board of Education itself had a computer of any type and decades before the PC became ubiquitous in schools. My Super Genba prototype worked.

McLuhan stepped in personally to support SEED in a powerful address to the Toronto Board of Education. Two years afterward, SEED became a full-time school and still exists forty-five years later. One of our students, Melissa Franklin, went on to become the first woman to get tenure at Harvard. She now chairs the Physics Department there and was a member of the team that discovered the Higgs Boson, the so-called "god particle," in 2012. Another, Jack Gruschow, created what is now Outlook and sold it to Microsoft. Today, he is building an industrial scale production system for renewable chemicals. Sara Diamond is President of one of Ontario's top universities, OCADU. Bonnie Fuller became the editor of *Glamour* magazine and *Cosmopolitan*, and is one of the most successful magazine editors in U.S. history. Cory Doctorow is a writer of best-selling science fiction.

SEED's Super Genba network-based school became the prototype for today's cloud-based universities like American Sentinel started by one of McLuhan's graduate students, Rick Oliver. ASU awarded me an honorary Ph.D for my work.

I built my first company, the publisher Northern Business Information, on the same Super Genba principle with Sean White, whom I met at the University of Toronto and with whom I've been in business ever since. McGraw-Hill, a Fortune 500 company, walked in the door one day and bought our company. Now I use the same concepts, much expanded in *Super Genba,* on companies around the world.

In its simplest form, the Super Genba structure is, like the SEED school, the fastest way today to move information within a company and between a company and its suppliers and customers. It has the added goal of turning that information into cash.

When I entered the University of Toronto as a freshman in 1969, I was invited to sit in on McLuhan's graduate seminar. Based on my new principle that information velocity is destiny, I determined to write the next chapter, as it were, in McLuhan's book.

The problem was that you couldn't just look up information velocity in a company annual report. Here, Sean White brought an essential piece to this analysis. In the early 1980s, as we were building Northern Business Information, he pointed out that the logical corollary of faster information is cheaper information. Our new rule: The cost of information is always falling. This is the force that expands the *genba*.

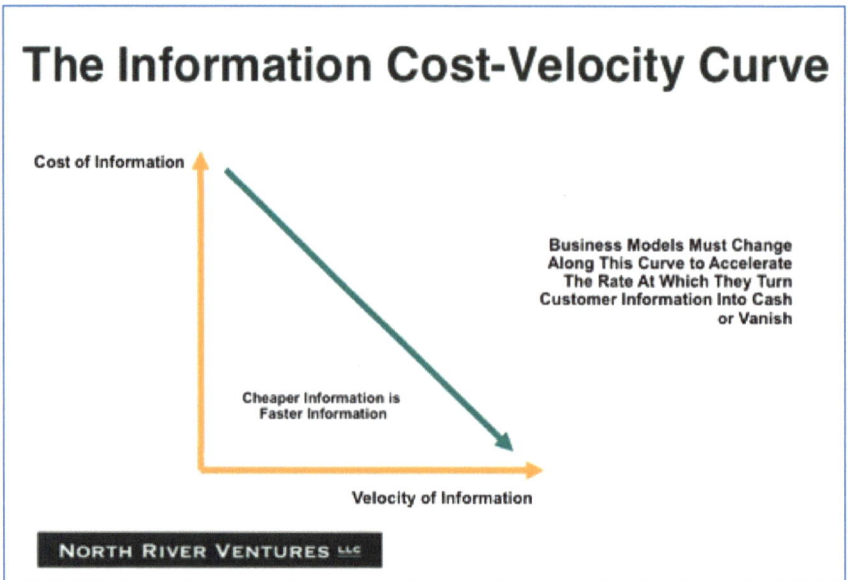

The Information Cost-Velocity Curve

Cost of Information

Business Models Must Change Along This Curve to Accelerate The Rate At Which They Turn Customer Information Into Cash or Vanish

Cheaper Information is Faster Information

Velocity of Information

NORTH RIVER VENTURES LLC

By creating an identity between information velocity and information costs, Sean made information velocities measurable, predictable, and therefore meaningful to managers. The Super Genba system in its detailed form shows managers how to take these measurements and turn them into actions that turn customer information fast enough to grow shareholder value.

The trick of survival for any organization from business to nation is how to move from *genba* to Super Genba as information costs fall. How do nations, for example, move from absolutism to constitutional democracy fast enough to stay on the falling Information Cost Curve? This is China's problem today. How do companies move along the Curve from vertically integrated corporations to cloud-based virtual organizations without falling apart? This is Panasonic's problem. Finally, how do they scale profitably in the Zetabyte Era of rapid Cloud Inflation?

Success in a *genba*-to-Super Genba transition comes from substituting ever-cheaper information for other resources like land, labor, and capital as the cost of information falls. Ricardo's comparative advantage today comes from how well you do this.

Failure comes from letting others use the information cost curve to substitute information for other resources faster than you do. No matter how effective it was in the past, your *genba* shrinks relatively compared to the competition and you lose. This is what happened to so many Japanese companies and why they fell so far behind so fast.

Different points on the Information Cost-Velocity Curve, and different rates of information substitution, require different business strengths. In the middle of the last century, cranking out lots of cheap product was congruent with the Information Cost-Velocity Curve as it then was. Manufacturing expertise—*monozukuri*—was the key differentiator. Japanese firms that excelled at this did very well.

Since that time, falling information costs have shifted market power from producers to customers—a process I will explain later—benefiting those companies that best control the *genba* rather than manufacturing. Today, all profit is made managing the selling process at the *genba*.

The transition from managing manufacturing to managing selling—which is what *Super Genba* is about—is not easy. Very few companies steeped in one tradition have ever made this transition. IBM is a notable success story and its transition was so difficult that a lot of people thought the company would not survive. But, IBM's transition was from one *genba* selling culture—it had always been *genba*-driven—to another. So you can imagine that the full transition from *monozukuri* to Super Genba will be very hard.

History and business textbooks are full of cases of how such *genba*-Super Genba transitions did not work. *The Wall Street Journal* lives off these stories. Rare are the examples of how it worked. Rarer still is the quantifiable standard for success that I provide here.

The question facing Lou Gerstner when he became CEO of IBM in 1993 was, can an IBM designed for the 1950s and 60s, when information costs were much higher than they were when he arrived, survive and have a profitable future? Yes, but at huge cost. Can an American Airlines outperform a Southwest or Jet Blue? Only by going bankrupt, as it did.

Can Sony, optimized for the 1960s and 1970s, survive to the 2020s? Howard Stringer, then CEO of Sony, wrote me in 2009 to say that he was fighting to restructure Sony to meet this challenge, "Sometimes I think I am winning, but I too wonder if there is time."

Your priority in solving your Super Genba challenge is measuring how fast you move information from customers through your ecosystem and turn it into cash. To do this, you need a set of indicators that shows how fast a company is turning customer information into value.

I use two measures—my Cash and Capital Velocity Indices, easy-to-use tools that I will define later—derived from corporate financial statements. *Super Genba* shows you can use these in tandem, like a car's tachometer and a speedometer, to shift your company's gears for optimum performance. And to calculate where you are with respect to your competition and customers.

Super Genba companies have high Cash and Capital Velocity Indices. These operations have high rates of information substitution, high information velocities, modern supply chains, good control over sales processes, low balance sheet loads, and outstanding increases in value and job creation. Super Genba companies are farther out on the Information Cost Curve than their competitors. They are at the leading edge of the cloud-based productivity revolution now sweeping the globe.

As we will see in *Super Genba* Step Three, the data show that only Super Genba companies can make innovation and top-line initiatives accretive. There is no example of a low-cash velocity company making innovation accretive, no matter how good the innovation is or how much of it there is. This explains why so many Japanese companies continue to stumble in spite of their technical prowess.

Super Genba shows you how to put your company at the leading edge of the cloud productivity revolution; how to run your organization for maximum growth and profit during a time when information costs are in a free fall and many competitors are being driven to the wall.

Staying on the Information Cost Curve means constant Super Genba reorganization and process innovation, something that Japanese companies have not fully understood. The result is that they have been frozen in organizational time somewhere in the mid-1960s. Trying to fast-forward half a century means changes that go well beyond the usual restructuring as Panasonic so painfully discovered. Changes this big stress management and require new tools. *Super Genba* is this tool. It is designed to move Japanese industry half a century in one move. While this may sound risky, it is much, much less risky than business as usual.

For Japanese businesses, the risks of remaining low-velocity *genba* operations in a high-velocity, Super Genba cloud world are unthinkable.

FALLING INFORMATION COST AND WEALTH CREATION

Ever-cheaper information allows us to replace other factor inputs with information, giving customers more for less. This increased information intensity creates what economists call a consumer surplus, money customers can spend on other goods and services, thus growing the economy.

Ever faster and cheaper information, therefore, is the *force motrice* of wealth creation. All wealth is created when the cost of information falls. This means that to be at the cutting edge of wealth creation, you have to be at the leading edge of the Information Cost Curve, and this where Japan needs to be.

By giving consumers more money to spend, consumer surpluses shift market power from producers to consumers. This is the mechanism by which information costs force producers to expand the *genba*. The more market power your customers appropriate, the bigger your *genba* has to be to profit from them. In our Zetabyte Era of rapid Cloud Inflation, your *genba* must be supersized and fast-inflating at cloud scale. Hence, Super Genba.

If the rate of information substitution for other resources is low, as it has been for most of history, the power shift and *genba* shift is imperceptible. History records the slow change in civil organization from Sumerian city-state to the empires of late antiquity and on through the emerging structures of China, Japan, and pre-Reformation Europe.

Even so, very small consumer surpluses driven by falling information costs can have dramatic effects if they are widespread enough. The combination of information and grasses unleashed the agricultural revolution, creating large amounts of wealth, changing human organization forever by driving the development of accounting and writing and the emergence of early city-states in the Middle East and Asia.

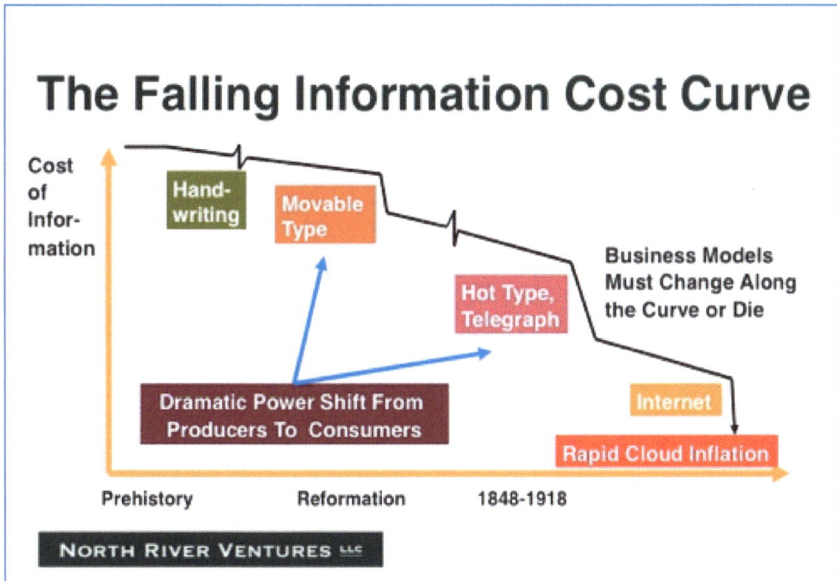

The Falling Information Cost Curve

If the rate of information substitution accelerates suddenly, as it did with the 1440 Gutenberg press and now in the Internet and Cloud Ages, it causes social, political, and commercial disruptions. This happened when paper communication accelerated the growth of Islam in the seventh and eighth centuries and again when a sudden drop in the cost of information initiated by movable type ignited the European Reformation in the sixteenth century. This is the kind of disruption that so many *genba*-constrained Japanese companies did not anticipate with the Cloud Revolution.

No European organization of any type survived the Reformation unchanged. Why would the Cloud Age be any easier to navigate? Why should your company do any better today than those medieval organizations that cruised into the Reformation blind and were crushed by it?

As every country that went through the Reformation found, each point on the information cost curve requires a different organizational structure and so a different sized *genba*. A *genba* design that works selling mainframes, for example, is unlikely to work selling personal computers. IBM discovered this to its cost and Dell to its profit in the 1990s, even though both sold computers. IBM and Dell sat on either side of McLuhan's "frontier between two cultures," as the old *genba* organization tried to compete with the Super Genba organization, and failed. IBM was a pioneer in computers and, through its market presence, built the PC market in the 1980s. But, in 2005, it sold its PC business to Lenovo.

If whole countries, like the Soviet Union, can evaporate by not adapting to the falling cost of information, your company can evaporate in a year or two.

Take Kodak. This company had distinct advantages in digital photography but elected not to go digital until far too late. It went under as a result. Why did management not move faster? Kodak's business model was film processing, a service. The cash flows and margins in this service business were far better than the margins in digital cameras, a manufacturing business with no film to process. Kodak decided to put off moving to digital in the mistaken assumption that it could preserve its cash flows from film processing in the face of the falling Information Cost Curve.

Kodak was so blind to the Information Cost Curve that it did not understand how its brand line, "The Kodak Moment" in which the word "moment" is read as a fond memory— preserved on Kodak film after time-consuming processing— could be delivered by someone else's digital camera and stored filmless on the cloud in a literal "moment," a fraction of a second. And sent to anyone anywhere in a moment as well. Kodak did not expand its *genba* to cloud scale. One of the towering brands of the twentieth century, Kodak is now history.

If your business model is unchanged since the TV age, which was a short time ago, it will not work in the Zetabyte Era. The two ages occupy very different places on the

Information Cost Curve. They are on opposite sides of McLuhan's frontier.

Super Genba rewrites *Das Kapital* to say that the revolution is not a shift of market power from capital to labor but a cloud scale shift of market power from producer to customer. While there isn't a capitalist among us who would agree with Marx's assertion that the tensions between capital and labor will inevitably result in revolution; there isn't a capitalist among us who would deny that in the Cloud Age there has been a revolutionary shift in power from producers to customers. Those whose *genba* inflated with the cloud profited from this neo-Marxist shift.

As many regimes in the Middle East discovered, even primitive cloud services like Twitter and Facebook can dissolve nations and governments faster than the press can report the story. The mission of *Super Genba* is to make sure this doesn't happen to you.

If information costs rise, as they did in the European Dark Ages and are now in North Korea, wealth is destroyed. Even if information costs decline at a relatively slow rate, as they did with the Soviet Union and are now in China, wealth is still destroyed. When the Information Cost Curve outran the Soviet Union—a nuclear-armed super power let us not forget—it vanished in a twinkling. Their relative position on the Information Cost Curve is what has hurt so many Japanese companies. They think that because every desk has the latest PC they are moving fast enough to add value, when, in fact, they are destroying it.

You can see China struggling with this as it attempts to benefit from the falling Information Cost Curve while preserving the power of the Party, which depends on centralized, high-cost information for its survival. To slow the rate of Cloud Inflation, the Party now restricts bandwidth to about six percent of the lowest rates that Verizon offers me at my home and 2.3% of Verizon's maximum bandwidth.[11] The idea that the Party can outrun the rate of Cloud Inflation is laughable.

In a nutshell, the challenge for management, and countries, is how to get ahead of the massive shift in market power to your customers driven by free falling information costs on the cloud and stay there. Doing this is all about having a Super Genba system big enough and flexible enough to maintain competitive position.

The great Konosuke Matsushita, of whom you know by now I am a big fan, would have taken this one step farther. During his early years, his advice to his company was to ride the wave of electrification that swept the world, and in his later years the wave of electronics, by making it easy for people and businesses to profit from these waves. Today he would say, ride the Cloud by showing our customers how to profit from it. And he would supersize his company's *genba* to make this work.

SUPER GENBA LESSONS

1. Companies must be designed inside and out to substitute information for other resources, like land, labor, and capital, as fast as the cost of information falls.

2. To profit from the power shift from producer to consumer driven by falling information costs, you must turn customer information into cash faster than your competition by super sizing your *genba* to cloud scale.

3. Comparative advantage comes from how well you substitute ever-cheaper information for other resources as the cost of information falls and the cloud inflates.

---

[11] Mozur, Paul, and Carlos Tejada. "China's 'Wall' Hits Business." *Wall Street Journal* 13 Feb. 2013

4. Failure comes from letting competitors substitute cheap information for other resources faster than you do.

How the Falling Cost of Information Impacts Business

Twenty-five years ago, Sean White and I were asked to advise the Canadian government on that country's high tech opportunities. We began by explaining how falling information costs affect organizations. To do this, we codified what we called The Iron Laws of Information in a tongue-in-cheek play on The Iron Laws of Wages proposed by the 19th century German socialist Ferdinand Lassalle. Our Iron Laws helped us explain the weaknesses we discovered in our pioneering work at NEC. We published them in *Beating Japan* in 1993.[12]

Business models, we said, are divided into roughly two camps: those that benefit from the Iron Laws and those that are its victims.

The Iron Laws of Information

The Iron Laws of Information draw from our own rule on falling information costs, Hubble's Law, the Second Law of Thermodynamics, and Gresham's Law:

1. The cost of information is *always* falling.

2. The rate at which customers appropriate power from producers is *always* directly proportional to the speed at which information costs fall.

3. Disorder in the information universe *always* increases.

4. Cheap information *always* chases out expensive information.

5. *All* the laws *always* operate simultaneously on any organization.

---

[12] *Beating Japan*, Francis McInerney and Sean White, Dutton, New York 1993, p. 276

You can see from the Iron Laws why, in 1994, we were able to predict with certainty that the marginal cost-based Internet would chase out the average cost-based phone network and disintermediate dozens of high-cost industries like music and book publishing, and retail stores.[13] Equally, we were able to ask, what does a viable business model in the new marginal cost-based world look like? Examining the early Internet companies, we were the first to conclude in 1998 that most hadn't a clue, that they were monstrously over valued, and that a stock crash was inevitable.[14] We alone showed when and why the 2001 Tech Crash would occur. Many stocks, like Microsoft, never recovered. Hundreds, perhaps thousands, of firms disappeared.

The Cloud Age spreads the Internet's marginal cost revolution from industry to industry at cloud scale, eviscerating many and giving others with successful marginal-cost based models dominance in the new order.

Yet, looking at the simplicity of the Iron Laws, it should have been easy for companies the world over to reach the same conclusions that we did and use the six years we gave them before the Tech Crash to derisk their operations.

As we wrote in *Beating Japan*, "The biggest challenge of the next century will be to exploit the Iron Laws successfully. For business this means ensuring profitability as market power moves to customers." Today, I would add to this sentence, "at the rate of Cloud Inflation."

In one sad case, I used the Iron Laws of Information to advise John Roth, the CEO of Nortel, then a $30 billion in sales a year telecommunications systems maker and customer of mine since 1978, that he had to prepare for a world in which toys as powerful as mainframes would

---

[13] *The Branding War*, North River Ventures LLC, July 1994
[14] *Internet Madness*, North River Ventures LLC, June 1998

dominate his markets. Nortel's customers, the world's phone companies, would have a hard time connecting so many powerful devices. If Nortel could help them overcome this deficiency and show them how to finance the process, it would assure their revenues, and Nortel's, for decades into the future. I demonstrated how this could be done, step-by-step. Roth told me in front of all his top managers that I was nuts. Nortel crashed soon after. Ninety-five thousand people lost their jobs and retirement savings. Investors were wiped out.

Of course, we are now well beyond the days of toys as powerful as mainframes because toys are now more powerful than mainframes ever were. Under the Iron Laws, all of this was logical and foreseeable well before the Tech Crash of 2001.

Which brings us back to the purpose of *Super Genba*. Using a few basic rules and a little common sense to supersize your company's *genba*, you can derisk much of the future and clear the way to innovations that add value for your customers for a long time to come.

FALLING INFORMATION COSTS AND MANAGEMENT

To profit from the cloud-driven free fall in information costs, management needs what Trotsky called a permanent revolution, a process of change which rolls on unceasingly. Smart CEOs, like Procter and Gamble's top boss A.G. Lafley, institutionalize this process.

Getting ahead of the information cost curve is a daily event. Yet, even though it should be self-evident that how you manage fast-falling information cost is the key to your survival, managers only rarely grasp this and often seem mystified as to why their operations are no longer generating the wealth they once did. But, just as Konosuke said, if you are not part of the wealth generation process, you have no function in the market, and will cease to exist.

In *Beating Japan*, twenty years ago, Sean White and I observed that only organizations designed along specific lines have internal velocities fast enough to turn customer information into value fast enough to get ahead of the falling information cost curve. Only these can harness the cost curve's centrifugal forces, and generate enduring shareholder value. These must be:

- Vertically and horizontally disintegrated
- Decentralized
- Flat, with no more than four management layers
- Designed to deliver customer service

This is a service-driven structure with all of its operations on the "surface" where they interact with customers directly. Today, I call this structure a company-on-a-cloud, held together on a server, a cash velocity engine with customers attached.

THE HUBBLE EFFECT

I named the Hubble Effect after famed astrophysicist, Edwin Hubble. It is one of the toughest things for modern business to manage. It is this: As information costs fall, customers move away from producers faster the farther they are away from them. And the greater will be the interstitial costs to producers, like inventories, with their effects on working capital and the bottom line. Cloud Inflation exacerbates the Hubble Effect big time.

The Hubble Effect says that anything that increases the distance between you and your customers will obey Hubble's Law. For example, the more layers of distribution you have, the more removed you are from your customers, and the faster they move away from you. Konosuke understood this better than anyone and never missed an opportunity to disintermediate markets to get closer to his customers. Japanese companies need to reexamine Konosuke carefully.

The Hubble Effect, therefore, makes intermediaries a high-risk factor. Disintermediation, by contrast, drives risks down. The auto industry in the U.S. is forbidden by state franchise laws from reducing these risks. Apple would not put up with this for a femtosecond. Curiously, most Japanese consumer electronics suppliers insist on value-destroying intermediaries and suffer greatly from the Hubble Effect.

Cloudless vertical integration, which is antithetical to cloud-based operations, increases the Hubble Effect by creating enormous distances from customers inside a company.

Another way of phrasing this is that the farther away from your customers your organization is on the Information Cost-Velocity Curve, the faster they are moving away from you.

However you look at it, the Hubble Effect is a killer. A business model that relies on cloud operations, direct sales, and maximum outsourcing will always overwhelm an old fashioned, cloudless, vertically integrated company that uses indirect sales.

Sometimes the embedded culture overwhelms this logic. I remember Kirk Nakamura in 2000-2001 urging Panasonic managers to focus on their core "black box" advantages and outsource or open source everything else to speed time to market, time to cash, and customer responsiveness. His managers got around this by defining everything they did as a "black box" and core to the company. This way they changed little. They outsourced some things but only a fraction of what he knew that they needed to. In English we call this "push back." After he retired, this push back cost Panasonic big time.

MANAGEMENT DECISIONS IN MOORE TIME

Moore Time is a measure of time on the Moore Curve. I created the Moore Time concept in 1995 to explain how fast decisions must be made when computer price-performance improves along the Moore Curve.[15] As Sean White and I explained at length in our 2000 book, *FutureWealth*, to keep ahead of the information cost-velocity curve, management decisions must be made in Moore Time.[16]

Today we have the added impact of Cloud Inflation. As we saw in the Introduction, the cloud inflates on three axes:

- The number of processors (growing exponentially)
- Times the power of those processors on the Moore Curve (growing exponentially)
- Times the power of the apps these support (also growing exponentially)

These three move in an underlying symmetry that I will explain later that affects just about every product and service known to man. The cloud subsumes all.[17]

With the advent of the cloud, the Moore Curve is no longer an interesting metric for the computer business. Moore Time forces all companies to manage ever-shorter decision cycles and ever-shorter cycles of customer attention. If your *genba* is not inflating with the cloud, Moore Time is a brand nightmare.

For obsolete *genba* companies, Moore Time means rushing new products to market while shelves are still brimming with "old" new products that must be sold off quickly in a

---

[15] *Black Holes and Dematerialization*, North River Ventures LLC, October 1995

[16] *FutureWealth*, Francis McInerney and Sean White, St. Martin's, New York, p. 34.

[17] Initially, I called this process The Big Bang. See *The Big Bang*, North River Ventures LLC, September 1996.

series of fire sales. Competing this way is expensive and wasteful. Add this to the cash wait states—inventories and receivables—built into the Hubble Effect and you can see how seemingly well-established businesses can vanish in a second.

As I explained in 1995, managing the Hubble Effect in Moore Time is essentially a problem of using the best IT to manage inventories and receivables, and therefore, working capital.

We have come a long way: McLuhan's "the medium is the message" is now "working capital is destiny." Both are about the same thing, managing the velocity and cost of information.

What has changed is that what McLuhan wrote more than half a century ago, and what Innis wrote decades before him, could not be translated into useful management tools. But everyone in the world who has so much as picked up an accounting textbook knows what working capital is and so can use the lessons of *Super Genba*.

Super Genba is all about setting working capital goals aggressive enough to force to the surface all the touch points of cash and interstitial costs in the Super Genba system. Understanding the relationship between cash touch points and Moore Time is the essence of Super Genba. Moore Time has a massive impact on how fast a company can turn customer information into cash. Miscalculate Moore Time and cash gets sucked out of your company, not into it.

The great genius of Sam Walton, and later of Michael Dell, Steve Jobs, and John Chambers, was figuring out how to cross McLuhan's frontier. They got around the "old" new product problem with innovative distribution strategies that slashed working capital loads, while their competition stayed behind.

A classic Moore Time miscalculation, as these executives understood, is grafting what companies take to be modern manufacturing techniques to legacy distribution systems.

Working capital loads go up instead of down, destroying the value of any innovation or top line initiative. This is a brutally hard lesson to learn and the core of what Kirk Nakamura tried to reform at Panasonic.

A mismatch between manufacturing and distribution, as Kirk realized, results in companies designed to push ever more of the latest products and services into an obsolete sales and distribution system that is layered with pools of inventory and cash wait states. Production velocity goes up, but information velocity goes down. Sales stagnate, and profits go through the floor. This was not the future that he wanted for Panasonic.

Competing in Moore Time is not about the speed of production or of product or service introduction, though many, especially Asian companies, think it is. It is about integrating manufacturing, production engineering, business development, marketing, service creation, and distribution into customers in one seamless Super Genba process designed to move the latest goods to market without leaving pools of inventory to be flamed off every time there is a new generation on the Moore Curve. As Yukio Nagira, CEO of Nitto Denko, likes to say, it is about selling functions, not products.

While value can be created in Moore Time—like the Internet Bubble of the late 1990s—it can also be taken away in Moore Time—the dot com collapse of 2001.

The Information Cost Curve shows this cycle repeated over the last half century as a series of explosive, Reformation-like events ripped into industry after industry. Note that:

- Each order of magnitude improvement in Moore Curve price-performance unleashes an order of magnitude increase in the number of processors. To get ahead of this, your organization must go into tomorrow's markets with tomorrow's organization.

- Toys are now more powerful and far more abundant than the PCs of only a few years ago.
- No company that was able to dominate one segment of the Moore Curve was able to dominate the subsequent one. Many have simply disappeared. This is Microsoft's challenge and Dell's. And it will be Apple's soon.
- Each order of magnitude increase in the number and power of processors places extreme pressure on business organizations. Many organizations are stressed beyond their breaking points.
- Half a century ago, mainframes existed at a ratio of one for hundreds of thousands, even millions, of consumers. Today, every man, woman, and child in the consuming world can have the power of many mainframes on many different devices, most of which are consumables.
- Thus, we are fast moving from a world of hundreds of millions of devices to tens of billions, all of which are networked at high speed on the cloud.

The next massive discontinuity is with us now: In 2006, IBM announced a 500 GHz processor which means that by 2016 we will see audio-visual devices of unimagined power in our pockets.[18] Business models must be designed today to tolerate the forces that will be unleashed tomorrow. And that we have known about since 2006, a century ago in Moore Time.

None of this is news in the computer business, where whole generations of top brands have been swept aside. NBC used an RCA computer for the 1960 United States presidential election. This early machine precisely predicted the outcome in one of the closest presidential elections in history, long before the final results the following day. Yet, most of those

---

[18] "IBM, Georgia Tech Unveil 500-Gigahetrz Chips" *The Wall Street Journal*, June 20, 2006, p. B3

in the computer business today have likely never heard of an RCA computer. Even the computer industry can misread Moore Time.

Market after market has been "infected" by Moore Time. Companies that have adapted to this have done exceedingly well. Walmart managed to turn a poor 2004 Christmas selling season into a winner because the President of the Stores Division had on his PDA, a predecessor to the smart phone, enough information from all stores by 8:00 a.m. on Black Friday, the day after the big American holiday of Thanksgiving and first morning of the Christmas sale season, to restructure the company's strategy and implement it system-wide within five days.[19] That was ten years ago. Even now, most firms wouldn't know what had happened, good or bad, until the season was over. That's the impact of Moore Time.

The IT that Walmart uses is prodigious and its time-to-cash benefits give the company the scale economies on which it keeps growing at $470+ billion in annual revenues.

Like it or not, businesses must have Moore Time information velocities, or die. The "or die" part of this proposition has come to haunt even high tech industries like telecommunications and computers. Many of the icons of the high tech age were structured for the past. History moved on and they did not. This is what has happened to so many Japanese companies.

Moore Time has several far-reaching impacts.

- Product cycles implode
- The cloud-based power shift from producers to customers accelerates rapidly
- Disintermediation, already a problem as customers use their market power to demand direct

---

[19] "Before Christmas, Walmart Was Stirring", *The New York Times*, January 5, 2005

relationships with suppliers over the cloud, becomes more accentuated

- Global brands become ever more difficult to manage

Combined, these impacts mean that a company that cannot operate at cloud scale in Moore Time will not simply under-perform the market; it will vanish.

SUPER GENBA LESSONS

1. Customers expropriate market power from producers in Moore Time.

2. Like water seeking its lowest level, ever-cheaper information seeks out the simplest environment in which to work. If management doesn't provide a high-velocity, low-cost of information environment, competitive advantages go elsewhere quickly.

3. Different points on the information cost curve require different rates of information substitution which in turn require different business models.

4. In Moore Time, even small relative differences in speed quickly translate into large losses of market share. For lack of a month, you can lose a Moore Time decade.

5. Make sure you understand what the falling information cost curve means *for your customers* before you make rash plans for the future.

6. Overlaying an obsolete business model on an information-efficient vehicle like the cloud will generate a value meltdown.

Use Super Genba to Accelerate Cash Velocity

Your biggest challenge is to create a *genba* big enough to turn customer information into cash faster than your competitors while information costs are in a cloud-driven free fall.

To begin, you have to know where you are on the Information Cost Curve. To do this, in 2002 I created two indices—of cash and capital velocity—that I combined to grade management.[20] If you have a low grade, you are too far behind the Information Cost Curve to scale profitably no matter what you do. You can have the most wonderful products in the world, but because you cannot turn customer information into cash at a competitive rate, you will go nowhere. You may even go out of business.

I described the Super Genba cash velocity system in detail in *Panasonic*.[21] The first thing to understand about my system is that there is nothing new in its fundamentals. All it says is that smart managers focus on three things:

- Working capital;
- Operating free cash flow; and
- IT tools for gaining superior results in both.

Super Genba companies have:

- A Cash Velocity Index (based on days of inventory plus days of sales in accounts receivable minus 40, a plug for days of cost of goods sold in accounts payable) of five or better; and
- A Capital Velocity Index (based on operating income as a percent of enterprise value) in excess of twenty.

I use an algorithm to combine these indices into company grades from A to F, with A being top of the class and F being

---

[20] *The Soccer Ball Company*, North River Ventures LLC, February 2002

[21] *Panasonic*, Francis McInerney, St. Martins, New York, 2007, p.91

a failure. Only top-grade companies consistently scale profitably. Grades also predict which mergers will be accretive and which won't be. Most mergers are between companies with poor management grades and fail as a result. Changes in grade standings are excellent predictors of stock market values, and you can track your grade on my web site, www.northriver.com, by hitting the Grade Your Management tab.

My Cash Velocity Index is easy to track and tells more about the internal health of a company than any gauge I can think of. I put in a plug of 40 for payable days because poor performers, like the European aerospace giant Airbus, which carries an extremely weak 220 or so days of sales in inventory and receivables, mask their operational failings by forcing suppliers to bank their businesses. This makes their operations look more efficient than they are.

The Capital Velocity Index is a measure of the efficiency of total capital employed.

Combined, these indices give a clear indication of how well management uses the two most important resources available: cash and invested capital. Work both these numbers well and your company will perform excellently regardless of most other factors. At the very least, the bulk of your strategic choices will be derisked, which means that you get to make more mistakes than your competitors. Put another way, you will survive mistakes that would kill your competition.

The Super Genba system is disarmingly simple. To run a company, management needs only a couple of measures that it can read quickly and understand. As the chart below shows, the goal of management is to increase sales while getting top Cash and Capital Velocities.

The theory is simple, but as *Super Genba* shows, the execution is complex. Do it right, however, and you create discontinuities in your market that allow you to extract disproportionate amounts of value.

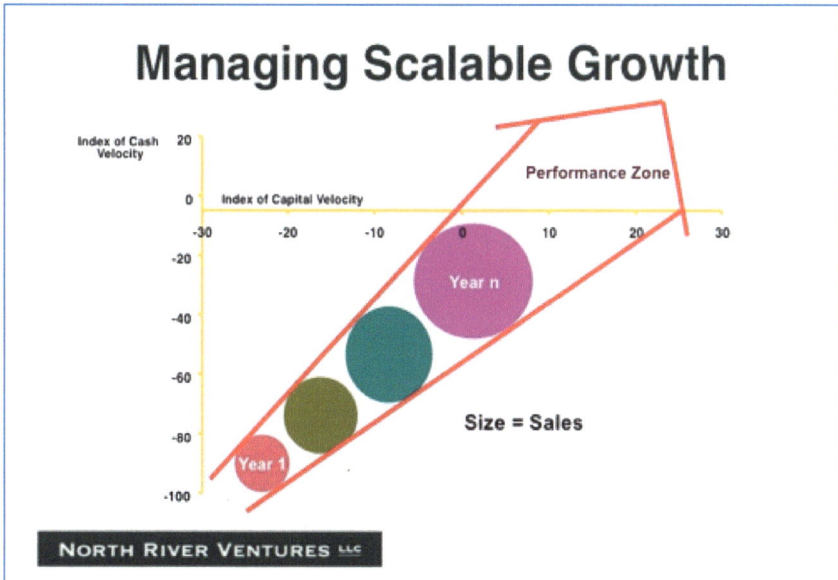

If you look deeply into my indices, you find that there is an unlimited set of operational impacts to these two measures. A good Cash Velocity Index means cutting inventory days, and it doesn't take much business experience to know that doing this will force to the surface fundamental questions about structure and cash management everywhere in the company's ecosystem every minute of the day, 24/7.

This is how Walmart, Proctor and Gamble, and Apple operate. Try to cut receivables to less than twenty days and you will soon see how much your sales force really knows about your customers. Show me a receivable cycle of 90 days—not uncommon—and I will show you a sales force that is completely inept and a top management team that has never met a customer.

Because the Super Genba System connects all aspects of operations to customers directly and increases information velocity between them, it governs everything you do from organization, operations, brand, finance, human resources, and customer service.

SUPER GENBA DIAGNOSTICS

We can learn a lot from examining the components of my Cash and Capital Velocity Indices. I use them to look into a company's operations and learn about its attitude toward customers and its ability to generate operating sources of free cash flow. Using these two indices, I lay out all the elements that are not working on the one hand, and, on the other, those that work well and can be leveraged successfully. Often this process finds hidden assets unknown to management that companies can better use, saving them time and money.

It always makes sense to reduce your working capital load. The closer you get to negative working capital, the better. Traditionally, working capital is a result of other actions and CFOs have few choices. If manufacturing and distribution systems pile on inventory, for example, the CFO's only choice is to go to the bank and push out payables, forcing suppliers to become bankers. These end-of-pipe solutions mask operating problems that could go on unchanged for decades.

What is different today, however, is that as information costs fall, C-Level managers can use IT to manage working capital data as cloud-born inputs. Apple, for example sets inventory days at three and structures its operations to fit that requirement. The only way you can do this is with top grade IT that identifies every inventory (cash) wait state in your ecosystem and eliminates these.

A company with good indices has superior control over the touch points of cash in its system. A company with poor indices has less control, or no control. Superior control over touch points of cash also means bringing in large amounts of information on customer needs and preferences that can be leveraged profitably throughout the ecosystem.

Walmart's understanding of its customers is legendary and gives the firm a proprietary advantage that covers the bulk of its global operations. Its *genba* is bigger than that of its competitors so it can compete from more parts of the ecosystem than others can. Walmart is well known for tracking major storms, for example, and filling its stores well in advance with what it knows that people in the affected areas will want before, during, and after the storm. Walmart's servers have a Big Data advantage.

When Hurricane Katrina hit New Orleans in 2005, Walmart had 45 trucks ready before the storm hit and sent a further 1,500 truck loads of food, water, and meals for 100,000 to the city in a few days.[22] Sadly, this prodigious Super Genba effort completely overwhelmed the U.S. Government's ability to distribute the supplies.

But, there is nothing Walmart does that is secret or even slightly mysterious. It just drives itself constantly closer to negative working capital with better inventory management systems. This allows a giant enterprise to keep scaling profitably as it has since its earliest days as a small shop in Bentonville, Arkansas.

As a rule, companies that do not turn customer information into cash quickly don't do anything very well. They are too operationally deficient. You can be certain that they have systemic problems with OFCF generation and that their IT is inadequate. My beginning point when I see this sorry state is Charles Mulford and Eugene Comiskey's excellent *Creative Cash Flow Reporting* (Wiley, 2005).

---

[22] Barbaro, Michael, and Justin Gillis. "Wal-Mart at Forefront of Hurricane Relief." *The Washington Post*, September 6, 2005, sec. Business

I look at inventory days first because they reveal operational issues that most people wouldn't notice. Anything over thirty days on a consolidated basis suggests deep problems with the supply chain, manufacturing, and outbound logistics, three big areas. It also suggests a low level of integration with customers. This in turn means the company is competing on price: It is selling its products at a discount rather than itself at a premium. It has built-in balance sheet and profit-and-loss deficiencies.

High inventory days show:

- Management doesn't know enough about its customers to show them how its own systems can reduce inventory days for both to create a working capital win-win. This means that the CFO, IT, and account management teams don't talk to each other very often. Look at your own data and then ask some questions. You will be blown away, believe me.

- The company has lost so much market power that it is suffering inventory blow back. Its customers are cutting their inventories at the company's expense, and management is learning to live with inventory bloat, never a good sign. GM's data said clearly as far back as 1999 that it would have to tear itself to pieces to reorganize. I published my predictions of a GM bankruptcy in February 2006.[23] *The Wall Street Journal* readers got the news three years later. You may be missing your own warning signs and losing large amounts of value.

- Management doesn't have control over operations, any idea of how to get control, or even what operations to control. This is an ugly unk-unk problem, the unknown unknowns that mean you have no idea about what you don't know.

---

[23] *Fixing General Motors*, North River Ventures LLC, February 2006.

- Poor connections between customers and the rest of the ecosystem, indicating a weak sales force, weak sales support, and anemic IT.
- Poor connections within the supply chain and no real time IT connecting the disparate parts of the company's ecosystem.
- Limited management understanding of the fundamentals of cash conversion and working capital management. No CEO is effective who does not immediately recognize that inventory is wasted cash. This means that the rest of management is ineffective as well.
- Reactive CFO operation—tries to fix problems after they occur—rather than active CFO management that identifies ecosystem cash wait states and shows line management how to eliminate these before problems arise.
- Weak management systems overall. Look especially for a poorly designed organization, a weak reporting structure, and inept managers. You can also expect to see a poorly formed review system, weak human resources management, and the promotion of the incompetent.

Low inventory days show:

- Management by cash wait state elimination.
- Strong IT linking all parts of the ecosystem worldwide.
- First-class sales operations well integrated with R&D, manufacturing, product development, and customers
- A well-disciplined team that understands what it takes to scale profitably and has the management systems in place to do this.

Then I look at receivable days. Again, anything over thirty days suggests problems in account management and also in billing operations and after-sales support. You will also find a systemic inability to support customer values directly, like selling on price when your customer really needs better yield rates, capacity utilization, and working capital. Or selling commodity consumer electronics when your customer is looking for better cloud access.

High receivable days indicate fundamental operational mismatches between a company and its customers:

- Account management teams are weak. In some companies I find no account management teams, just sales and service sales teams. These companies are forced to take the worst terms from their customers because they know little about their customers and can offer little.

- C-level conversations with customers don't exist, or exist on an unproductive basis. Nortel suffered enormously in the tech crash of 2001. It had more golf outings for customers than Ai Miyazato has daily practice shots. But when I recommended that Nortel's talking points should be all about generating customer OFCF, I was told that its customers wanted to talk only about Nortel's products and prices. Nortel no longer exists.

- Top management doesn't have the skills to sell into customer value sets. I find this problem all the time. Selling cash and showing a customer how to get closer to negative working capital is something too many managers know nothing about and they cannot say how their own products and services do this.

- Excessive use of distributors and too few direct sales to understand how the market and customers work.

- Lack of consumer and business ethnography.

- Sales by discount, ceding all the profits in a market to better managed competitors.

- Nonexistent brand, or, as I like to call it, brand in name only.

Low receivable days show:

- High level of operational integration with customers with all the IT that it takes to do this.
- A great deal of customer information that the competition is not getting and therefore the likelihood of hard hitting competitive moves into markets others don't yet see and are ill-prepared to enter.
- Deep integration of customers into all levels of company upstream activities, like R&D.
- Premium pricing.
- Top-flight brand management of all aspects of the customers' experience of products and services.

The third element of cash velocity is days in payables. Inefficient management commonly masks poor inventory and receivable data by stringing out suppliers. This makes working capital look good without fixing the problem. In fact, it makes the problem worse: It cannot possibly be good for a company to suck all the cash out of its supply chain. This just makes the system weaker, not stronger, and increases the likelihood of predation and/or collapse.

To understand how this works, read Apple's annual report to see how it uses its working capital advantages to use payables strategically. Apple uses the superior IT that drives its low inventory and receivable days to map demand for key components well into the future. It then locks down supplies of these by prepaying for them long in advance.

Competitors with weaker working capital data don't have the IT to see demand into the future, and by the time they get to that future, they find that Apple has locked up all the supply of components they need. If they can get these components at this late stage, they must pay a premium. In 2008, Ben Verwaayen, then CEO of Alcatel-Lucent, complained to me that he was having a hard time buying components because Apple appeared to have soaked up the market. He was paying for having a low cash velocity system and I told him so. He did not fix the problem. By early 2013, sales had fallen 15%, the company had lost €7.6 billion, and Verwaayen lost his job.

For companies that don't believe in spending on the latest IT, Apple's kind of thinking is not available. The competitive losses because of this are beyond measure. Sean White and I first showed how IT gave cash-driven companies huge competitive advantages over cost-driven ones in early 1995, almost two decades ago.[24] Super Genba-managed companies work on the assumption that the working capital health of the entire system is essential. Low cash velocity companies don't care and probably don't know that they should care.

Finally, I look at velocity of capital. Here is an example.

Nokia had great capital velocity a few years ago and so-so cash velocity, meaning that it was what Michael Dell calls a "pool of cash" waiting to be siphoned off by a competitor with superior working capital management.

Apple, by contrast, had great cash velocity but so-so capital velocity, positioning it to strike hard at Nokia and others with innovative, premium products (as it did), and to do so repeatedly and with impunity.

I used the Super Genba system to call attention to this in April 2006, years before the market grasped what was happening to Nokia.[25] Today, we all know that Apple ran over it like a truck. The cost to the company and its shareholders was enormous. By 2013, sales were down 40% in five years. Nokia traded at $15 at the end of 1998 when Apple traded at $10. On the day of my warning, Nokia traded at $21. In early 2013 Nokia was off 86%, trading at

---

[24] *Walmart and the Falling Information Cost Curve* North River Ventures LLC, February 1995

[25] *Nokia Warning*, North River Ventures LLC, April 3, 2006

32% of sales. Apple traded at $450, or 2.6X sales. Nokia since vanished into Microsoft.

This is really no different from what happened to so many in the Japanese CE sector. Like Nokia, all these companies had huge advantages that they did not press and lost almost everything.

There is nothing secret in any of this. All the data are available in annual reports and take only a few minutes to enter on a spreadsheet. You can, within these few minutes, use my guidelines to see your strengths and weaknesses. From this it takes only a short time to create an action plan. When CEOs call me, I usually have all the data I need before the first meeting.

When you know that a company has poor cash velocity, for example, problems jump out that would not have been obvious on a factory tour. Some are really simple to diagnose. Like asking an LCD factory manager how long it takes to make an LCD—a day and a half. Then asking how long it takes to ship LCDs to market from Japan—between four to six weeks—and that is only to the point of system assembly. Then ask why the company went to such lengths to pile up weeks of inventory. Most LCD factory managers have not thought of this, probably because they are not measured on it. They focus on capacity utilization and yield rates, neither of which helps them compete with someone who runs an equally high quality global operation on three or four days of sales in inventory.

Shortly after his appointment as CEO of Philips in 2001, Gerard Kleisterlee and Philips CFO Jan Hommen invited me to Amsterdam to explain the fundamentals of my system and what it would mean for Philips. The result was a decade-long restructuring that continues under Kleisterlee's successor.

Sometimes, there is a dark side. During a presentation of my system one of the line of business boards at Siemens, a top executive piped up with one of the oddest statements I have ever heard: "We don't need Francis' system to control the touch points of cash because I have it on good account from our customers that they are prepared to pay us a premium for our products." What I thought was even more odd was that no one else in the room jumped on his head for such foolishness. Not long after, we all discovered why. This division had been paying large bribes to customers and my cash-driven system would have exposed this immediately. The company paid a $1.6 billion fine, a doubly expensive way to run a low-cash velocity operation.[26]

Companies that manage cash and capital velocities well have so many customer touch points that they achieve Brand Superiority, the ability to affect outcomes in their markets that we will discuss later. These companies are hard to displace from this position because of their operational virtuosity.

THE SUPER GENBA ZONE SYSTEM

To help you use *Super Genba* to create your future, I use my Zone System as described in detail in *Panasonic*.[27] This is the system Kirk Nakamura used to guide his restructuring of Panasonic between 2001 and 2006. I will give you a quick review here.

The Super Genba Zone System shows how competitors rank in the race to turn customer information into cash. Kathy Matsui's team at Goldman Sachs used my Super Genba Zone System in 2007 to identify Japanese winners. After some penetrating research, Matsui's team concluded, "Japanese firms need to focus on raising cash velocity."[28]

---

[26] "Press Release: SEC Charges Siemens AG for Engaging in Worldwide Bribery; 2008-294; Dec. 15, 2008," December 15, 2008.

[27] *Panasonic*, Francis McInerney, St. Martins, 2007, p. 119

[28] *Cash Velocity: Identifying Winners*, Goldman Sachs November 21, 2007.

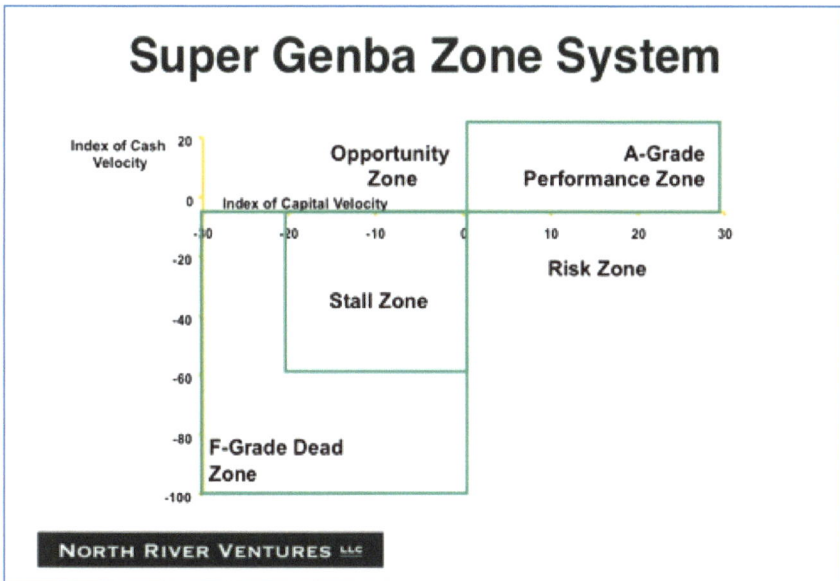

Super Genba Zone System

NORTH RIVER VENTURES LLC

Goldman's clear warning came half a decade before the huge losses at the companies that Goldman said were vulnerable. The only possible explanation for these setbacks, therefore, is management failure on a gigantic scale.

Matsui's team concluded that low-cash velocity was the primary reason why Japanese consumer electronics companies would not be able to come up with an iPhone.[29] This was only a few months after Apple launched the product. Goldman showed that it was clear as glass to anyone using my Zone System that, as soon as the iPhone hit the market, Japanese companies would not be able to respond without altering their business models from one end to the other. They did not alter their business models and got the expected results.

Let's review the Zones.

---

[29] *Why Japanese Manufacturers Cannot Come Up With An iPhone* Goldman Sachs, September 14, 2007

THE DEAD ZONE

The Dead Zone is the graveyard of the modern corporation. Companies here have lost control and have little internal cohesion. It is where F-graded management goes to die.

I advise CEOs in the Dead Zone to set very aggressive goals in inventories and receivables and to drive these personally. Everything else, I tell them, should be delegated.

They will not have time, for at least a year and maybe two, to deal with new products or top line initiatives of any kind. I tell them that any top line initiative taken while in the Dead Zone could kill off the company, just as Compaq's acquisition of DEC forced it to sell itself to Hewlett-Packard and then drove H-P into over a decade of trouble. Executing a merger when in the Dead Zone is a premeditated form of market exit.

Dead Zone companies often have dead corporate cultures: people with no initiative and no hope, who plan at best to hang onto their jobs and wait for retirement. In companies like this, even the best CEOs have a hard time pushing for change. The inertia is just too great.

THE STALL ZONE

The Stall Zone is the hardest to manage of all the zones because this is the place where management's internal consistency is most tested. For incrementalists—managers who make a career out of tweaking a number here and there to achieve conservative goals—the Stall Zone is home. Here they can keep operations on a more or less even keel, so long as no Performance Zone Super Genba competitor enters their markets.

If this does not happen, Stall Zone companies can turn in respectable performances for prolonged periods, keeping shareholders content, though not happy, and most important, allowing managers to keep their jobs and all their perks. In many industries, like the automobile industry, under-performers survived for decades only because their competitors were so much worse. When the 2008 Crash hit, though, the weaknesses that I foresaw for the auto sector in 2006 became apparent quickly.

For most executives, it is only human to get to the Stall Zone and go no farther. This Zone does not require them to break the mold the way Lou Gerstner did at IBM and, while they work hard, of course, their *manque d'imagination* is not penalized. They work for their salaries, and shareholders take the hit on value.

Inertia makes it so hard to cross the Stall Zone to the Performance Zone that the biggest risk to firms in this Zone is that they will fall back into the Dead Zone. Time and again I find companies whose management just doesn't have the stuff to make the transition. No matter how hard it is to do, getting from the Dead Zone to the Stall Zone is a just small part of what it takes to get to the Performance Zone.

As at Panasonic, which fought its way from a Management Grade F to a C- under Kirk Nakamura's aggressive reforms, Stall Zone companies have yet to make the biggest decisions in their histories. This hit home hard after Kirk retired. Panasonic's new management simply folded, pushing the company back into the Dead Zone from which it is beginning a long struggle to re-emerge.

If a company decides to get inventory days from a Stall Zone thirty to a Performance Zone three, for example, its entire ecosystem will have to be reinvented, as will its customer interface. That is most of the company.

THE RISK ZONE

Companies in the Risk Zone have a combination of a high velocity of capital and a low velocity of cash that tells predators that they are easy, profitable hits.

This zone is for Michael Dell's pools of cash. These pools spin off lots of operating earnings but do not have the cash velocity strength to compete with Performance Zone companies. This makes them attractive objects of predation for companies whose first class control of the touch points of cash gives them superior information about customers and markets and the means to turn that information into cash faster than Risk Zone companies.

Risk Zone companies, like Microsoft, can survive for extended periods, however, if they have a proprietary lead in their markets. But once their sector becomes commoditized, or rendered obsolete as Microsoft now appears to be, they quickly become victims of companies with higher Velocities of Cash.

Dell and Walmart both made their mark by spotting Risk Zone companies and dismembering them. Nokia found itself in the Risk Zone, under easy attack from fast-rising Samsung and Apple among others. In spite of having a dominant share of the cell phone market worldwide, it was reduced to rubble in only a couple of years. Management promptly went into a crisis. Nokia's market share and core financials went into a tailspin.

In Nokia's case, its lack of customer information allowed it to tell itself that it was a cell phone pure play. Apple, with a cash velocity high enough to drive far more customer information into its product development, recognized instead that it was in the business of managing cloud access across multiple platforms, only one of which is cell phones.

Apple then moved to secure dominance in several cloud platforms from PCs to tablets, cell phones and TVs, appifying industry after industry. Doing this, it simultaneously eviscerated the business models of dozens of companies in dozens of markets, including Nokia's. Nokia could have done the same thing. Caught in the Risk Zone, however, it had little customer information, could not see its own market, was caught in a cell phone prison, and entered a painful downward spiral.

The Opportunity Zone

Opportunity Zone CEOs need to ask hard questions about what they are doing with all the customer information they are getting. Companies like Walmart do not let a single piece of customer information go to waste. The trick in the Opportunity Zone is to recognize that you are in it and then focus on leveraging your customer information into earnings.

Opportunity Zone companies can launch new products more safely than most outside the Performance Zone. Apple was a classic. It used its Opportunity Zone position for years to clobber the competition with iPod and iTunes, soaking up OFCF and growth, a nice double play. Then it moved into the Performance Zone.

Apple was able to define the iTunes/iPod market to its own specs, turning a commodity MP3 format into a proprietary lake and dominance in the global recorded music industry. It then extended this lake through a steady transformation over several platforms from PCs to tablets, phones, and TVs on the iCloud. Competitors with weak cash velocity operations tried to counterattack with products, which is impossible, and were killed off.

Smart CEOs get to the Opportunity Zone quickly. There, time is on their side. They have the market high ground and can carefully survey the competition to see where and when they should hit. And when they hit, they hit very hard, propelling their companies into the Performance Zone.

The Super Genba Performance Zone

Performance Zone Super Genba companies share one important benefit: they gain Brand Superiority (see *Super Genba* Step Five). They impact their markets rather than respond to them. By controlling all their cash touch points as well as they do, they have incomparably more customer information than their competition and can turn this into cash faster.

Because their competition does not know that so much customer information exists, Performance Zone companies take all of it for themselves without the slightest response from the competition. This is what happened to the once-mighty Japanese consumer electronics sector. Companies in this sector let others take in all the customer information in their markets and then sold into a vacuum, with predictable results.

It is amazing how different customer information is between those companies in The Performance Zone and those outside it. Dr. Hartwig Rüll, formerly of Siemens, studied this question using my Super Genba model. Hartwig's work shows that well-managed customer information often allows Performance Zone Super Genba companies to inflate themselves on *all* the operating free cash flow in their markets.

Hartwig demonstrated that Performance Zone companies with high cash velocity improve their ratios of operating earnings to R&D over time while firms with low cash velocities must struggle just to stay where they are and usually lose position over time. This finding was a real eye opener for me and explained why so many companies outside the Performance Zone have a progressively harder time competing over extended periods. Their options diminish continually, even if they maintain the same management grade.

Hartwig's research shows that after only five years, Performance Zone companies are so far ahead of those outside the Zone that their R&D coverage is 65% better. He makes a persuasive case that once your company is in the Performance Zone, competitive advantages accrue at a faster rate. He shows that these companies get much higher:

- EBIT margins
- EBIT/Inventory ratios
- OFCF/R&D

- OFCF/SG&A
- Return on Assets

Super Genba Performance Zone companies get higher ratios of OFCF to R&D and OFCF to other SG&A at the same time. They get to both innovate profitably and sell those innovations profitably. This win-win is the core of their ability to scale.[30] It is also the reason why Performance Zone companies destroy more value for others than they create for themselves. For all the value Apple built for itself, the amount it destroyed for others is much, much greater. Performance Zone companies aren't just competitors like all the others. They are killers.

Hartwig's point is that it is not only easy to foresee who has the best chance to win and lose, it is also easy to predict operational outcomes at a highly detailed level. Performance Zone companies have none of the same risks as their competitors and as a result can make very different decisions. Apple for years took over 50% of the profits in smart phones on only a tiny amount of market share, just as Hartwig predicted.

Companies like Apple look at the Performance Zone in the right way. They tighten up operations to gain top-grade Cash Velocity Indices. This puts them into the Performance Zone from where they can attack in their chosen markets at will. These companies are much less vulnerable to predation when they are at their weakest: launching untried products into untried markets, something that regularly sinks Dead Zone, Risk Zone, and Stall Zone companies.

The biggest risk to Performance Zone companies is that they fail, as Dell did, to take advantage of their position and allow others in this Zone to out innovate them. This is because, as we shall see later, innovation is enormously accretive for companies in this Zone in a way that it cannot

---

[30] *New Market Drivers*, North River Ventures LLC, November 27, 2007

be for others, for whom innovation can often be extremely negative.

Kathy Matsui's team at Goldman Sachs added to this by saying that the business models used by Japanese companies were not at all comparable to Performance Zone winners and that they suffered as a result. Earlier, I called this the process of markets breaking into high- and low-grade dyads.[31] The results can be dramatic. You have to look no farther than the 2008 Crash to see how A Grade companies suffered almost none of the ill effects of low grade ones. For Walmart there was no Crash. But for Metro it was devastating. Hartwig's case study comparing Cisco to Alcatel-Lucent over the last decade is eye popping. He shows that once the performance gap opens, it tends to get wider over time, and, as we know, this cost Alcatel CEO Ben Verwayeen his job.

We will spend the rest of this book on why this should be and what you can do about it.

How Apple Manages the Performance Zone

In Japan, everyone, except those who supply Apple, tries to dodge the Apple question. In consumer electronics, for example, the Japanese focus on Korean competitors, like Samsung, which suffer from the same cloudless thinking from which Japanese companies suffer. By comparing themselves this way, they miss the point. Apple has devastated market after market for a decade and a half and has yet to face a real competitor. This makes no sense. Why focus on Samsung at the back door when Apple has just blown off the front of your house?

Steve Jobs liked to say that his company did not do market research. In saying this he was not being entirely honest. As a Performance Zone Super Genba company, Apple's whole

---

[31] *Market Dyads,* North River Ventures LLC, June 29, 2007

system is a Big Data sponge for customer information, a market research powerhouse in its own right.

As I wrote in the Introduction, I've been in meetings in Japan where product managers offered streams of data showing that sales in all their markets except Japan were declining for years. They think something is wrong with overseas sales staff and asked me to recommend changes.

When I explain that all these products have vanished into Apple's maw and that a single iPhone does everything that all their products do and has over 850,000 other apps into the bargain, managers commonly say, "But the iPhone is not a quality product like ours."

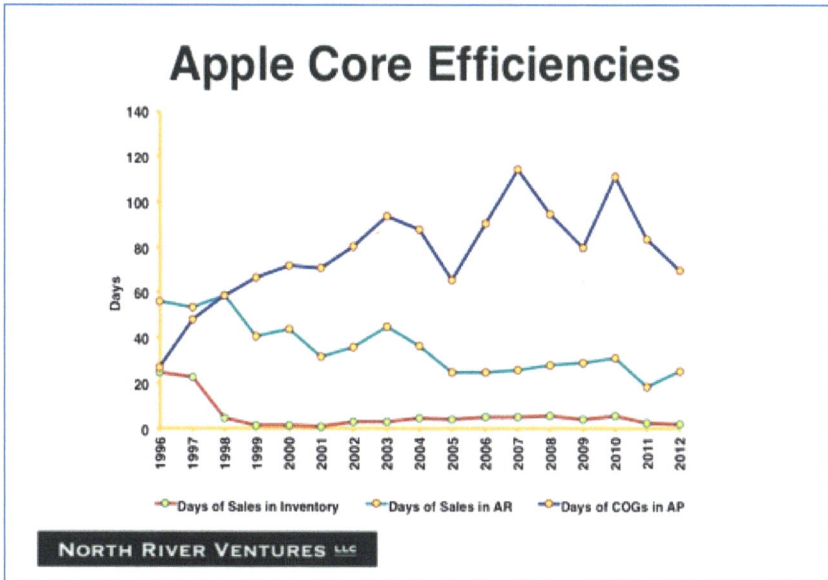

Unfortunately, their customers don't agree. Apple's Big Data allows it to understand this and profit from it.

Let's start with Apple's numbers. You can see on this chart that when Steve Jobs returned to Apple in the late 1990s he brought with him a new cash velocity-driven business model and an operational genius to execute it, Tim Cook.

80

The new model focused on lightening the balance sheet to the point where it became a strategic tool. By 1998, days of sales in inventory were cut to five. They are now three. The company multiplied sales 26 times by 2012 and profits 212 times. By flat-lining inventory days, Apple took a small number of products that you could lay out on a modest boardroom table and put itself in a position to hit $200 billion in annual sales. That's scale economics the way Japanese companies should be thinking.

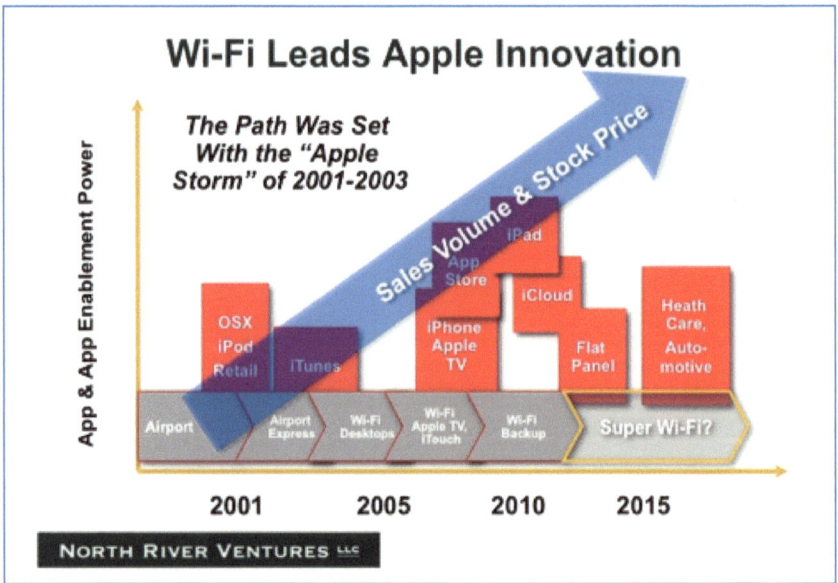

Wi-Fi Leads Apple Innovation

As we saw earlier, Apple uses its balance sheet power to prepay for components that it foresees that it will need sometimes years in advance. This way, Apple preempts much of the market. But, as Jobs said, anyone could do this.[32]

Apple has combined simplicity of operations with simplicity of product. On the next chart you see that during a twenty-four month period between early 2001 and early 2003, in

---

[32] http://allthingsd.com/20100607/steve-jobs-at-d8-the-full-uncut-interview/

what I call the Apple Storm, the company launched every platform that made it a world-beater for the next decade:

- Airport Extreme (Wi-Fi)
- OS X (now with iOS)
- iTunes (now iCloud)
- iPod (now iPhone, iPad, and iTV)
- Apple Retail

All Apple products are designed to fit onto Wi-Fi and iCloud backplanes, positioning the whole portfolio to inflate with the cloud as simply and quickly as possible. The company has not deviated from this strategy in the decade since by so much as a Planck Length. While its competitors wandered all over the place trying product after product—think of Nokia's problems and Blackberry's—Apple combined its operational efficiency with a simple goal for its customers, to manage their experience of the cloud seamlessly across all its platforms. And to turn the information that results into cash faster than any competitor.

Apple sells cloud management for many products. Its competitors like Hewlett-Packard, Lenovo, Nokia, Panasonic, Samsung, Sharp, and Sony, still think that they are in single markets like cell phones, TVs, or computers. They treat each as distinct products with separate manufacturing and sales silos. Apple recognizes that this is a mistake. There is only one business: managing how customers interact with the cloud. Products are the result of this; they are secondary, not primary.

This is the reason Apple went to war with Samsung over the physical interface that customers touch. The screens of the iPhone and iPad are Apple's cloud gateways. They are far more important to Apple than anything in the devices themselves or, probably, on the iCloud servers. All the apps in the world are great, but it is what happens when its customers touch Apple's screens that makes cloud management work. That is the magic to which Jobs so often referred.

For Apple to double in size to $400 billion, the size of Walmart, and again to $800 billion, it has to grow in markets big enough to generate huge sales. There are two: health care and automotive. Zensorium's Tinké shows already what Apple might look like in health care: a powerhouse able to consumerize expensive procedures, slashing the cost of medical services in any place that touches the cloud. Which means, everywhere.

Zensorium, owned by Nitto Denko, shows Hyper Monozukuri at work: Nitto polymers as a real time health care gateway to the cloud. At the touch of a finger you can track your cardiovascular health with Tinké plugged into your iPhone anywhere in the world at any time. I like to challenge friends to beat my numbers. (Because I walk seven kilometers a day at one kilometer every ten minutes, this is hard to do!)

For the multi-trillion-dollar automotive market, you know with certainty that there is a team in Apple working on an iCar. This will be an iPad on wheels. I recently bought a new Audi and was horrified to see how badly its instrumentation was arranged. The GPS is a nightmare to navigate and the phone and satellite systems are primitive at best.

Apple already hosts many auto apps. Waze is a favorite of mine, and you can see in Waze why Apple went to such lengths to push Google's maps off the iPhone. And why Google bought Waze to add value to Google Maps. Expect Apple logos on the front and back of cars all through your neighborhood.

Google has the same ambition and already has driverless cars on the road. Google and Apple have plenty of cash to fund these ventures.

What future does Toyota or Honda have once iCars and Google cars hit the street?

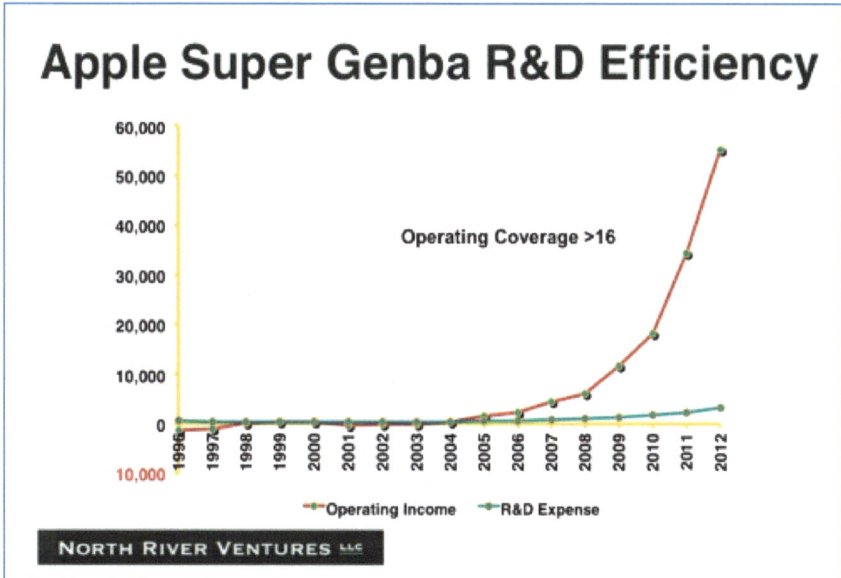

Apple's and Google's main barrier to entry in cars is not technological. They can have their cars made by any number of companies just as Foxconn makes iPhones. The barrier comes in a surprising place, retail. Like all car companies, Toyota is forbidden by law in all of North America from selling cars directly to customers. If Apple had to sell products this way, it would never have had the success it has had. Car dealers siphon off all the valuable customer information and send it nowhere. Carmakers, as my Audi experience shows, have no idea what customers want. They proceed on blissfully as if the Apple Storm of a decade ago had never happened. This is asking for trouble.

Should Apple gain the right to sell iCars the way it sells iPads, it will suck all the profit out of the automotive market the way it has in iPhones where it takes some 50%+ of the profits for a small percent of the market. Android phones have a significantly larger share than iPhones but no one is making much money selling them or their apps.

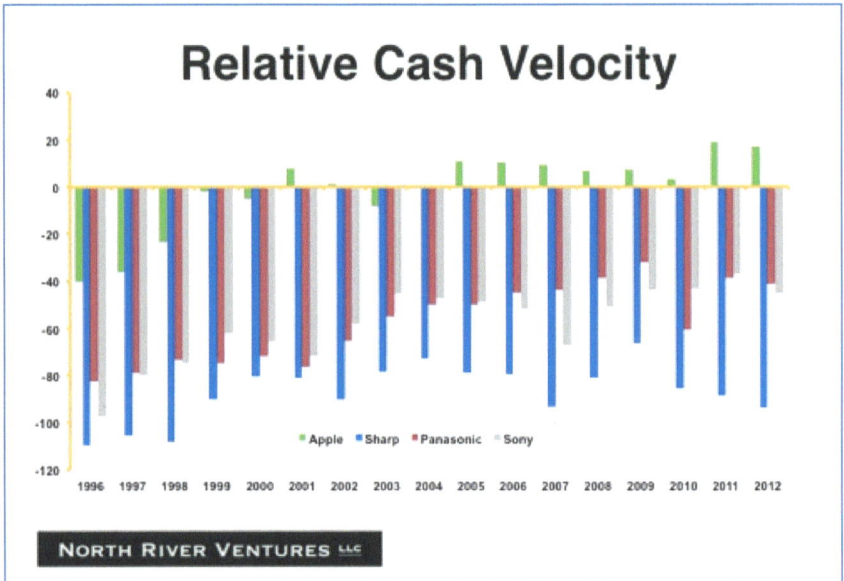

What should also terrify Apple competitors is its stunning R&D efficiency. Right after the 2001-2003 Apple Storm, this took off. There are many Japanese companies that have not seen Apple's 2005 ratio for forty years and more. I call this the "Edison Gap" (see *Super Genba* Step Three: Manage Innovation), the shortfall between R&D and operating earnings that occurs when centralized R&D, in the century-old Thomas Edison style, stops scaling.[33] Check the data to see how many Japanese powerhouses have recovered their R&D any time in the last quarter century. The answers are jarring.

This leaves many Japanese companies vulnerable to an Apple charge into markets where Japan already leads—automotive—or wants to lead—health care—sharply reducing Japan's growth options.

To see how easily this could happen, let's review what happened in Japan after Steve Jobs returned to Apple.

---

[33] *The Edison Gap*, North River Ventures LLC, August 16, 2007

You can see above how three big Japanese names compare to Apple over a period of sixteen years, long enough for any one of them to have changed direction and prevented their dismemberment by Apple.

The most obvious thing in the chart is that Sharp either did not think about its operations or chose to ignore all the data in its own annual reports. It does not matter which because either one is deadly.

In 1996 when its stock peaked at ¥1,780, Sharp had 59 days of sales in inventory and 90 days of sales in receivables, for a total of 149. This said that its supply chain and sales operations were completely out of control. To mask this enormous deficiency, it held 138 days in its accounts payable.

By 2012 Sharp had 78 days in inventory, meaning that its supply chain was even worse than 16 years previously and 55 days in receivables, a real improvement, but not even close to where it needed to be because the total was 133 days, better by a mere sixteen days in sixteen years, or one day a year. Any manager looking at these data would never have invested in the $11 billion Sakai LCD factory.[34] As I predicted it would, Sharp wound up in trouble and subsequently off-loaded Sakai onto a joint venture with Hon Hai. Between 1996 and 2013, Sharp's stock fell 77%.[35]

At Panasonic you can see attention to cash velocity during the 2001-2008 period, and at Sony from 2007 to 2011. But none of these companies was focused hard enough on Apple, which was bearing down on them full speed and had been since Steve Jobs return in the late 1990s.

To top predator Apple, the absolute measures on the previous graph do not show their real value. When I recast

---

[34] Wakabayashi, Daisuke. "Sharp's New Plant Reinvents Japan Manufacturing Model." *The Wall Street Journal*, December 1, 2009
[35] *Not So Sharp,* North River Ventures LLC, October 9, 2009

these data on the next graph to show relative positions, they show Apple's Moore Time advantages. Even though Panasonic improved its cash velocity quite a bit during this sixteen-year period, it wound up farther behind Apple in 2012 than it was in 1996. Sony remained in the same position, and Sharp deteriorated markedly. These data explain all the troubles in which all three found themselves in 2012.

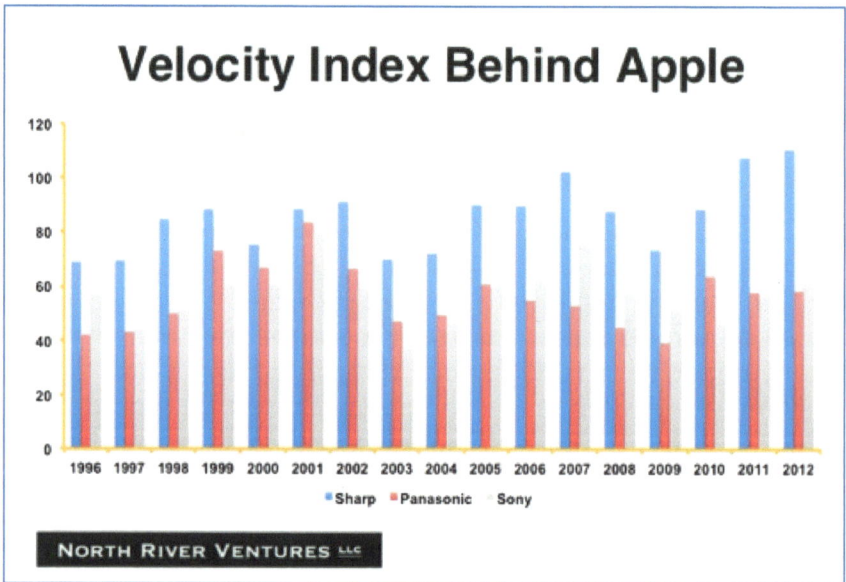

Velocity Index Behind Apple

So, no matter how much these companies improved in absolute terms, at the end of the period they found themselves no better off with respect to Apple. Sharp found itself much worse off.

Let's say we were to map these companies' cash velocities onto the "Apple Curve," the rate at which Apple improved its cash velocity during the first five years after its decision to focus on this key management metric. It should take the best performing company on these charts—Panasonic—six years, or 2018, to get to where Apple was in its 2002 fiscal year. But only if it applies the Apple system immediately. This means that in the most optimistic case, Apple has a decade and a half advantage over Panasonic. Any delay would increase this advantage. Sharp, which is so much farther behind, would have to act at several times the speed of Apple, something no one has done. Goldman Sachs was right to be alarmed.

This is the impact of Moore Time. What looks like a theoretically manageable combined 60 days of sales in inventory and receivables, for example, translates into a Moore Time disadvantage of decades. Similarly, during the same period of time, Performance Zone top predators make strategic decisions while their prey in the other zones can only make tactical decisions. Japan's Performance Zone competitors make more and bigger decisions more quickly and can move farther and faster in every planning cycle.

When I came up with the concept of Moore Time in 1995, I was able to demonstrate for the first time the material impact of McLuhan's frontier on business models and how companies like Apple make decisions.[36] Competitors that could not act as fast would be crushed. Which is exactly what happened.

Now turn this around and imagine that we are Apple, looking at these data a decade and a half ago. We would realize immediately that the field is ours for the taking. The data said unambiguously that we could expect no response from our competition. We have all the time we need. History proved Apple's judgment correct.

Anyone operating with these principles, as Apple does today, can rest comfortably knowing that under the most favorable circumstances competitors will be unable to respond for between ten and fifteen years, an insuperable advantage, and hugely tempting.

---

[36] *Competing in Moore Time* North River Ventures LLC, August 1996

Another frightening thought is that, as I said earlier, companies like Apple, and Dell before it, destroy more value in others than they create for themselves. The companies that Dell erased from personal computing with its direct sales system never came back. Even though Dell faded as other business models superseded it, the companies it destroyed, like Compaq, did not return. The same is true of Apple today. If it were to vanish tomorrow, the damage is already done.

One of the reasons that Japanese companies so often miss their markets is that, if you think COGS-driven *monozukuri*, you cede all your competitive advantages to your high cash velocity, Hyper Monozukuri competition. I have been told more times than I can count that Japanese companies are *monozukuri* operations, that *monozukuri* is their core DNA, and that it is the line on which they will fight. To which my answer is, that's fine, but don't expect your customers to care very much about your DNA. They only care about themselves. Your high cash velocity competition is getting to these customers first and managing them for profit.

When Howard Stringer, then CEO of Sony, first read my thinking in "Japan Must Reinvent Monozukuri Or Die" in August 2009, he wrote to me, "I read your article with a mixture of fear and trembling but nevertheless with appreciation and admiration. Your analysis is spot on."

PART TWO: THE TEN STEPS TO SUPER GENBA

SUPER GENBA STEP ONE: USE THE CLOUD

By giving the most remote person or thing access to unlimited computing power at marginal cost, or zero, cloud computing is the biggest event in history. This cost discontinuity is so powerful that it is sucking in everything. No one, no company, no state, and no thing can resist the power of unlimited computing at marginal cost.

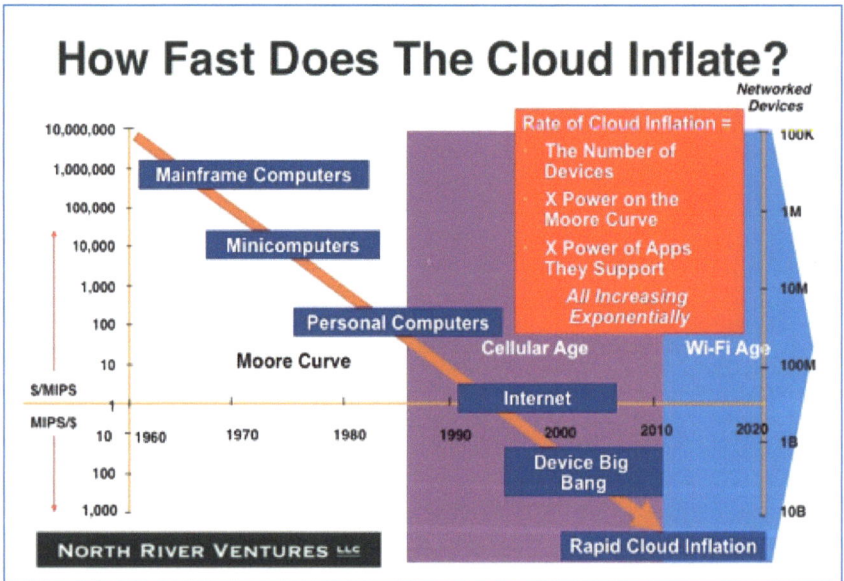

The cloud substitutes low cost information for other resources like land, labor, and capital at a rate that makes the sum of all past revolutions, industrial and political, look like a sideshow. Nothing this big has ever happened to us. The cloud will dominate our lives for the foreseeable future.

Clouds are a simple and logical next step on the Moore and Memory-density Curves. They are the biggest information velocity accelerators we have ever known, marking a break with the past more profound than even the Gutenberg press of 1440. Managing clouds will take a lot of adjustment, nowhere more than how we structure our companies to scale profitably.

We know well that the devices we use are more powerful by the day and that there are always more of them. This means that the cloud is dynamic. As I wrote earlier, it inflates at exponential rates along three axes at once: the number of processors times the power of these processors times the power of the apps these processors will support.

Combining these three axes make the size of the cloud imponderable.

Here is an example of the impact of Cloud Inflation. I'm an avid golfer. For my iPhone I got a $29 Golfshot GPS app for mapping the course and tracking my play. This inexpensive app far outstrips anything my $349 Skycaddie can do. Golfshot GPS improves itself automatically with the power of the cloud. To get a better Skycaddie, which is bigger than my iPhone, has only one function, and is nearly as difficult to use as a TV remote control, I have to replace the unit for another $349, and pay an annual subscription of $50. But, my iPhone has access to another 850,000 apps besides Golfshot GPS. At this rate, Skycaddie should pay me to use its products!

I am now getting desperate e-mails from Skycaddie begging me to "come back."

Golfshot GPS shows not just the powerful scale economics of the cloud, but also impact of Cloud Inflation. Two years ago, Skycaddie was the thing to have for tracking your golf round. Most golfers I know had one. Today I see iPhones. The cloud has inflated fast and far enough that Apple is in the golf business.

This is the same thing that happened to Japan's CE sector. Fast moving cloud-based products designed to exploit every part of the Apposphere subsumed endless numbers of stand-alone, unappified products, like cameras.

It is now a basic rule of business that the structure of all organizations must inflate with the cloud.

Cloud Inflation brings to our daily life something that quantum physics deals with every day: Heisenberg's Uncertainty Principle. This says that you can calculate the velocity of something or its location, but not both. If you get accurate information about how far the cloud has inflated, you can never accurately gauge the speed of its inflation. And vice versa.

What should you do to manage this? I advise managers to imagine they are standing on the cloud looking out. What, I ask, do you see? The answer is, everything. Medical devices in people's bodies, cars, schools, energy systems, factories, ships, planes, mines, almost anything you can think of. There is nothing that is not a function of the cloud. Or will be.

From this, two things jump out.

First, clouds are an everywhere and everything phenomenon. They are everywhere your customers are and in everything they do. If you are cloudless, you are irrelevant to them. Selling modern products means selling cloud services first and products to which they are attached second. The value is in the cloud.

Second, smart managers don't scale their factories; they scale their companies with the cloud. As in the Sharp and Panasonic examples, you don't build one giant LCD operation because you think that there are production economies in doing this. You ask instead, what does the cloud allow me to do? Answer: Cloud mechanics allow me to keep a maximum of five days of sales in inventory by distributing my LCD manufacturing close to major markets. The next question is how to use cloud servers to optimize capacity, yields, and supply chains in each of those locations and use them as load levelers for other locations.

Put the two together—cloud ubiquity and industrial scale on the cloud—and we have the core of modern industrial organization. To have Super Genba, more action with customers in more places, we must be clouded. We cannot reach enough customers fast enough, nor turn what we learn from them into cash quickly enough, without making the cloud our central organizing principle. The cloud is the core of the organization's ability to inhale customer information and turn it into cash fast.

Unlimited computing at marginal cost will, like a giant black hole in cyberspace, pull in everything. Nothing will escape it. Cloud access will become universal for all people, organizations, and devices, no matter how remote, no matter how big or small.

This makes the cloud the Gutenberg Moment of our time, a massive cost discontinuity that will reorder far more than business. It will reorder society worldwide. Productively harnessing this force is the primary mission of businesses worldwide.

Clouds are the modern day version of Konosuke's "tap water philosophy" (水道哲学) by which consumer electronics should be cheap enough to flow into homes like tap water. The cloud revolution allows computing power to flow in the same way.

In the past, we thought of products and markets—like consumer electronics, industrial machinery, transportation, and medicine—as distinct, each with its own operating procedures and rules of supply and demand. These products dominated the pre-cloud, product-driven, tap water world.

We also thought of software as something that ran a single product, like a server, or a PC, or a network of them, running an application, like accounting. Films were films, and computer operating systems were computer operating systems. The industries that made them were unrelated.

Finally, we thought of networks like telephone, cable, and cell nets as separate infrastructures with their own needs and investment cycles that had little to do with markets for

consumer electronics, films, cars, or factory automation
software.

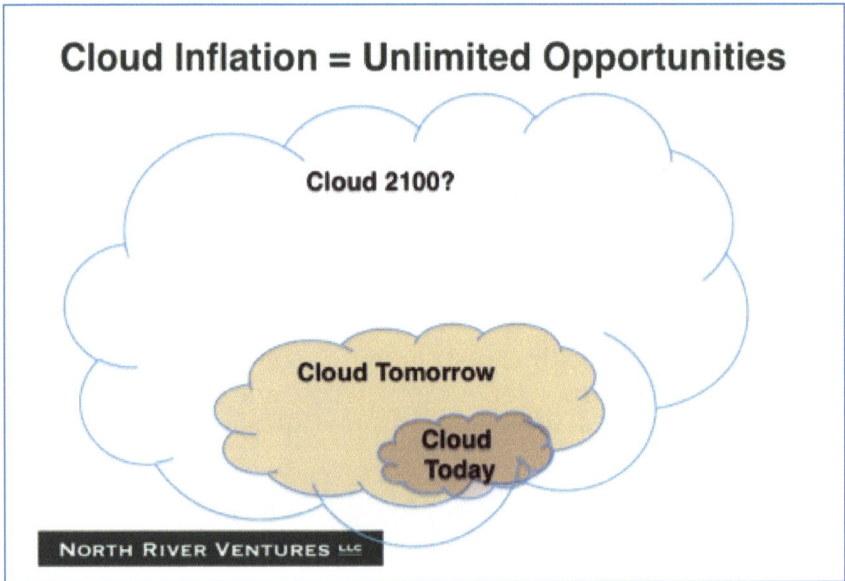

On the cloud, by contrast, all these things, as diverse as they
may appear, are part of the unified field of the Apposphere.
Either they enable apps, deliver apps, or are apps themselves.
No more and no less than that.

On the cloud, all products are functionally the same no
matter how unlike each other they appear to be. An appified
refrigerator sits equally on the cloud next to a cell phone or a
fuel cell. All the independently designed and operated
devices of the pre-cloud world have only one function today:
enabling cloud-based apps the same way that a smart phone
does. To the cloud, a hospital is a giant health care app
enablement device (AED) just as your cell phone is a small
one.

Today, therefore, we see a soup of cloud-driven AEDs, all of
which are indifferent to each other on the cloud. Just as
McLuhan predicted for his world of "electric-all-at-onceness,"

on the cloud, there is no near and no far, no specific geography, and no specific function. Clouds are any and all phenomena.

Just as the cloud is indifferent to devices on it, cloud apps are indifferent to each other. As with the Golfshot GPS example, clouds already manage hundreds of thousands of apps with distinct functions and business models. Neither the cloud nor the devices on it really care which is which or how they are used.

This, in its simplest form, is what Steve Jobs grasped faster than any other industrialist. Looked at this way, he understood that on the cloud Apple could leverage anything it does indefinitely in any market. Like an iPhone with an ever-increasing number of apps in an ever-increasing number of markets and with a platform that can move horizontally into TVs, cars, tablets, computers, everything. It also means that Apple can potentially expand its sales at the rate of Cloud Inflation, something no one had done before. Konosuke would have understood this instantly.

Given the Moore and Memory-density Curves, it is already impossible to distinguish between cloud servers and AEDs: Your smart phone is now powerful enough to be my server.

Moreover, when we take into account the potential for the Moore and Memory-density Curves to enable machine-to-machine cloud interaction, the number of AEDs in the future is imponderable. We can safely say that, by 2020, the Moore and Memory-density Curves will unleash at least one hundred billion app-enabled devices way more powerful than today's PC. All will be self aware and able to communicate a great deal about themselves.

Finally, there is the third piece of the cloud world: how all these things communicate. Since Cloud Inflation and indifference set the rules for apps and AEDs, they must also set the rules for the systems that connect them. The communications system between devices and apps must inflate at the rate of the cloud to carry its zetabyte loads and beyond.

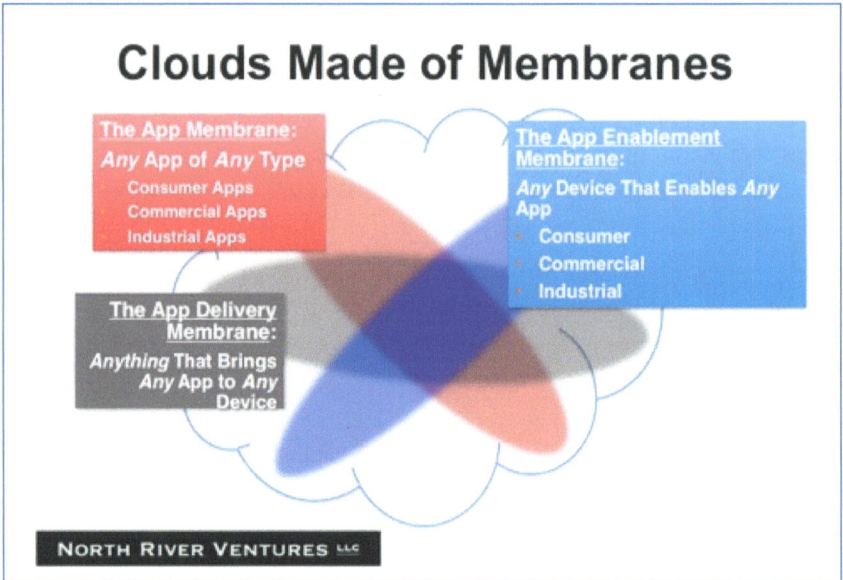

This complex cloud world needs a new lingua franca so that all participants can understand what is going on and how the parts interact. At the Corporate Innovation Project that Sean White and I run at North River Ventures in New York, we invented one.

This language lays bare the economics of a Hyper Monozukuri company like Apple. Adopt this language, which is really very simple, and the futures of dozens of industries from media to factory automation, health care, automotive, and energy management become clear. Using this language, you can understand how Apple sees these markets, why it has exploited so many so successfully, and what Japanese companies can do to profit in the same way.

Our Corporate Innovation Project formulation starts, as I said, with our observation that, in the cloud world, everything is part of an app soup that we call the

Apposphere. It enables apps, delivers apps, or is an app itself.

From this we concluded: The cyber cloud comprises three fluid and changeable membranes.

The cloud membranes are:

1. The App Enablement Membrane, which includes anything that can be connected to a cloud whatever it is, in whatever market

2. The App Membrane, which includes all cloud apps regardless of industry or market or where they are hosted or used

3. The App Delivery Membrane, which includes anything wired or wireless that connects AEDs to cloud-based apps

Importantly, as subsets of the cloud, the membranes share all its characteristics.

The membranes:

• Have no limits, like our universe, though they are not infinite

• Are driven by the Moore and Memory-density Curves

• Can intersect one another in any combination, and re-intersect in any combination. There is great value in knowing the most profitable of these intersections and being the first to get there

• Have no predefined shape; they can include anything, anywhere

• Inflate with the cloud itself

98

We used the word "membrane" to force everyone to understand that the cloud is both shapeless and inflating in many directions and markets simultaneously. We also want people to understand that while each cloud membrane expands on the Moore and Memory-density Curves, each is also driven by the inflation of the other two membranes. Under Reed's Law, moreover, the utility of the cloud scales exponentially with respect to the size of each membrane.[37] This gives the membranes huge scope for growth and, as Apple saw, as complex though as membrane expansion and interaction is, it provides many opportunities for profit. Cloud membranes are the sales doubling scalars of Super Genba.

Monozukuri and the Collapse of Scale Economies

In most of the industrial age, customers sat on the left side of the picture below, and saw only unrelated stand-alone products, such as TVs, cars, healthcare devices and many other things. Vendors focused on products one-by-one, often adding many versions in an effort to find the market's sweet spot. But, offering dozens of cameras for a single unappified function, photography in this example, made economies of scale hard to achieve consistently.

The result was the earnings-deflating cycle of product proliferation typical of many Japanese companies. Many are so fixated on this cycle that they don't see that they are on it. In one case, right after saying that a new product was unnecessary, a company launched a whole new generation just because it saw a competitor do this. The company's customers did not fit into this calculation. Huge losses resulted.

---

[37] Formulated by David Reed, see:
http://en.wikipedia.org/wiki/Reed%27s_law

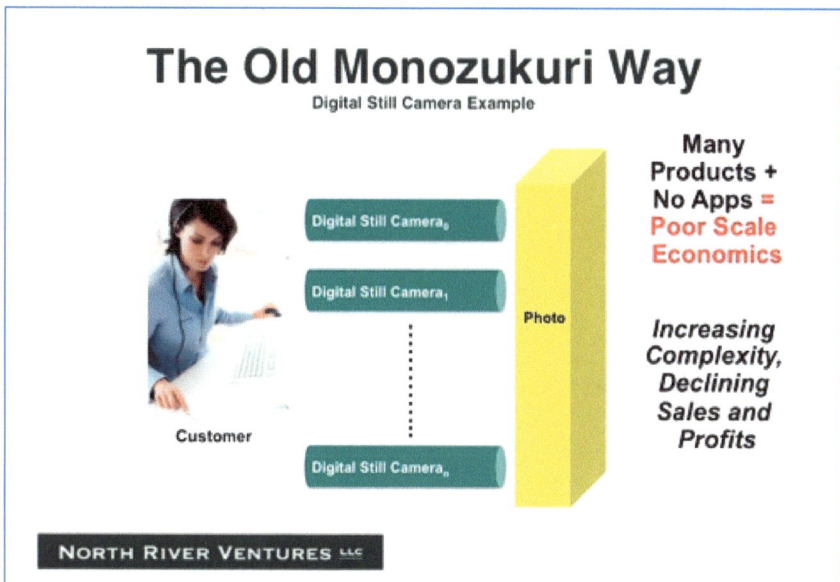

Monozukuri-driven product proliferation is the direct result of deficiencies in customer information. The only reason that a company might offer, say, fifty digital still cameras, most of which cannot possibly be profitable, is that it does not have the customer information it needs to offer the one or two models that customers really want. It does not have the cloud-based system or the basic ethnography to get this information.

In one curious turn of events, NTT DoCoMo requires its Japanese cell phone suppliers to replace products with new ones every few months, long before the old products have a chance to be profitable or successfully introduced on the world stage. It claims that this is what customers want. Yet Samsung and Apple are exempted and offer new products in Japan on their own global timeline, and for their slowness they dominate the Japanese smart phone market with a combined 96% market share.[38] Clearly, DoCoMo has not the slightest idea what its customers want!

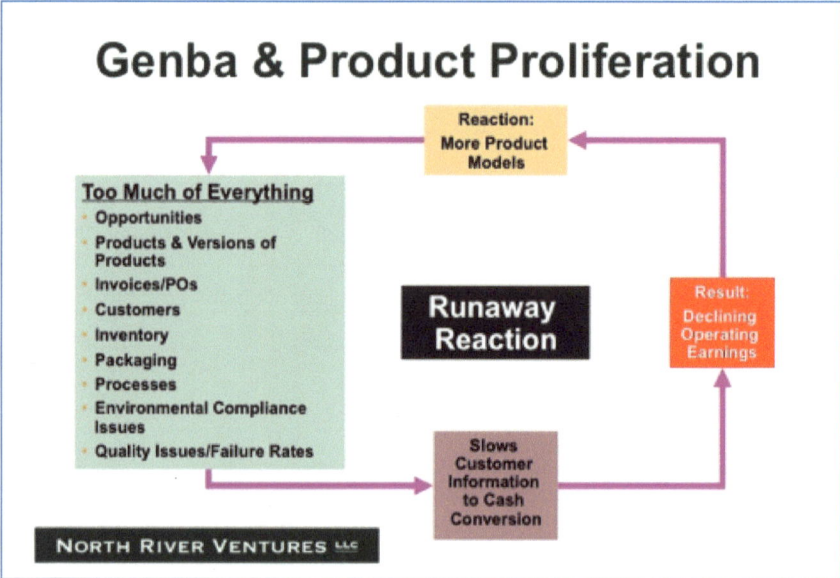

If product proliferation were the only problem that results from lack of customer information, it might not be so bad. But its follow-on effects are costly. Look at the next chart. Under "Too Much of Everything," you can see large negative impacts on both income statements and balance sheets, a double hit. You can be sure that a company in such a situation is impossible to manage; things are far too complex.

On my first day visiting a new B2B client in Japan, a proud factory manager took me around his plant showing me all the products made there. It was obvious to me within a few minutes that so many products hid a large number of problems that were slowing this company down and killing its ability to scale profitably. Sure enough, I soon saw a

[38] Tabuchi, Hiroko. "Fad-Loving Japan May Derail a Sony Smartphone." *The New York Times*, June 26, 2013

ludicrous amount of expensive packaging waiting for all the products, a certain sign of both inventory and yield problems adding to a supply chain nightmare.

The factory manager bragged that the number of invoices going out to customers had doubled over a recent period. I was horrified: I want to see bigger sales and fewer invoices. Instead, the company was creating more and more products with smaller and smaller sales potential. It had no idea how profitable, or not, each of these products was.

I worry more about the balance sheet impact than profit because I know that companies with few days of sales in receivables and inventory also have great cost control. Fix one and get both. The reverse does not work, however, because it does not reveal root causes in the system. Sure enough, this company's days of sales in receivables were much higher than those of its top competitor, indicating that the sales force had few modern selling skills and that manufacturing operations had not been integrated into customers Super Genba style.

The answer to this company's problem is to create Super Genba Global Account Management (GAM) operations (See Super Genba Step Two: Drive Sales) to drive customer information into product development in real time. By doing this it can cut unnecessary product proliferation and accelerate cash velocity.

A GAM enables business ethnology. We need to study our customer's operational and product problems, show customers how to fix both, and make more money than planned. Apple's iCloud does this for consumers across 850,000 apps. That is putting the "Super" in the *genba*.

CLOUDS AND THE NEW SCALE ECONOMIES

In the cloud world, the "Old Monozukuri Way" chart is reversed with profound consequences. Customers sit on the right side, as in the next chart, where they see apps, sometimes hundreds of thousands of them, not products. How you manage your customers' experience of these apps is the alpha and omega of Super Genba brand management. As many companies discovered to their cost over the last decade, if you manage only the products on the left of the chart, you manage nothing. In New York we call you "fish food." As in, the Mob bumped you off and your body is deep in the ocean feeding the fish. By ignoring the shift of Konosuke's tap water philosophy to the cloud, much of the Japanese CE sector became fish food.

Apple was the first to understand that in all future markets, cloud membrane interaction will be primary and product secondary. As Apple was also the first to understand, a simple, cheap, and flexible communications medium like Wi-Fi, not cellular, is the key to linking apps to app enablement devices.

So, how do clouds alter scale economies?

- Cloud Inflation is an unprecedented growth phenomenon

- The ability to mix and match AEDs and apps anywhere, any time, so as long as the App Delivery Membrane is as cheap and flexible as Wi-Fi, means that you can adapt quickly to a large range of markets

- The primacy of apps means that one AED can support many applications, cutting R&D, manufacturing, and other SG&A costs

As Apple discovered, apps have their own cloud-like logic. This logic needs careful attention because in the three-membrane cloud world it determines all outcomes.

On the cloud, an app is just an app and, as on a smart phonesmartphone, it can appear in any order without respect to its function or business model. This app indifference gives unprecedented flexibility and allows customers to optimize product features any way they want.

Equally important, the same app can appear on any media interface from cell phones and their offspring to computers, M2M devices, and the soon-to-arrive 8K video panels in homes and businesses worldwide.

Also, apps are unlimited in context, power, and function. Some could be a few lines of code; others could be as data-heavy as computer games or medical apps in 3D8K video.

This app logic applies to all apps no matter what their function or content, from B2B to B2C, from entertainment to automotive, and education to medicine or energy management. Such common logic allows companies to launch any product in any market on the same principles, simplifying product planning, branding, manufacturing, account management, and many other functions. But, to profit, industry must first grasp the significance of app logic on its products.

As they do on a smart phone, no matter how differently they operate, all apps look the same, making them appear to be functionally equivalent, irrespective of their embedded business models.

This functional equivalence creates a form of app identity:

- Entertainment apps = healthcare apps = automotive apps = energy management apps

Super Genba says that on the cloud you can use this identity to mix and match your own or anyone else's apps. You can leverage unrelated products on a single platform, a clear scale benefit.

Any customer can access any app, anywhere, any time. Customers determine app usage exclusively, and app developers have only limited control over this. In the app world, customers worldwide can operate on the same, or different, principles, as they choose and when they choose. Localization is inherent in the app so that less has to be designed into the hardware to meet local needs. Another scale benefit.

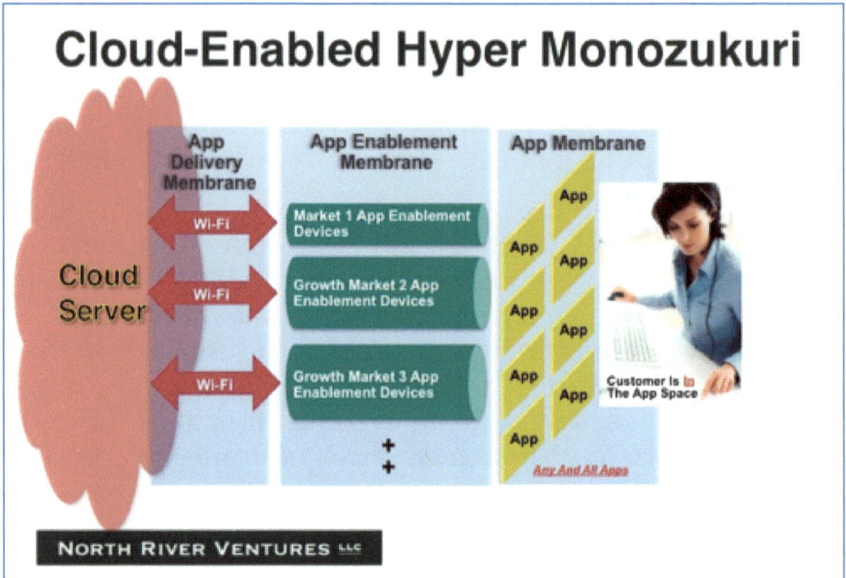

In spite of their appearance of functional equivalence, however, apps have embedded business models that are noncontiguous and may vary widely.

To see why this is so helpful, contrast apps with standard linear media, like TV. We can think of TV as something like a roll of analog film with individual TV shows embedded as picture frames. The film roll is the advertising-based business model and the frames in it must follow this model in the time sequence to which they are assigned. If one show fails or is put in the wrong time slot, it often puts the future of a whole channel into question.

Apps are the exact opposite. While they appear similar on the screen of a cell phone, each app has its own time sequence and does not have to follow another app or relate to other apps in any way. You can place them on your smart phone or any other App Enablement Device in any order that you choose. Unlike a TV show, if one app fails it has no impact on the others because there is no TV channel in which they are forced to coexist.

Because app revenue models are kernels inside the app shells that you see on a smart phone or a tablet, each app revenue model can be independent of all the others. Yet these models can be mixed and matched at will, just like the apps that carry them. This can be done for any industry, B2B or B2C, in any market.

This business model variation means that neither you nor your customers are stuck in only one way of doing business. You can quickly drop what no longer works and replace it with what does and do this in different ways for different locations and applications. Today's 3DHD on-line game app, for example, could morph into tomorrow's 3D8K health care or automotive or electric grid management app. App logic says that this is inevitable. As the cloud inflates, it sucks in more and more businesses.

Here is an interesting Nitto Denko polymer example of just how far the process of appification can go. Shale oil recovery requires large amounts of water, often in areas with little water to go around, making water very expensive. A set of forward osmosis water recycling systems at each oil well when connected on a cloud server can allow oil companies to monitor water consumption and reuse at any number of wells anywhere in the world to the second. This not only cuts the cost of oil recovery but, because forward osmosis increases oil recovery rates, it increases revenues too. So, appify forward osmosis membranes on a global scale and everyone makes money.

Better still, you can derisk app development and slash the cost of product development, both big scale enablers. As with Apple and Google, your customers can develop their own apps with unique business models, load them onto your app cloud platform, and make money by selling these apps to other customers. This way, as Apple found, the bulk of the risks of app development falls on the app developer, not the owner of the app store. If an app succeeds, you win. But if the app fails, you do not lose. Another scale benefit.

In this Hyper *monozukuri* process, customers, rather than manufacturers, differentiate products and create the secular shifts in demand that open new markets, taking on much of the cost of product development that was once born by the manufacturer.

For example, tablet customers opened a large new market in education that Apple did not anticipate when Apple's customers populated their iPads with many of the apps needed to drive this large market. Apple quickly jumped into education with iTunes U. As soon as Apple launches a new product, new markets like this pop open on Apple's iCloud servers like cherry blossoms in the spring. All at no cost to Apple. That's the new scale economics of the cloud.

App users lead where they want to, providing you with market after market long into the future. By creating the new applications needed for your new markets, your customers raise barriers to entry for your competitors. Before the cloud, this kind of risk sharing for mutual benefit was almost unheard of outside of expensive and capital-intense projects like resource development. App stores like Apple's and Google's make this scale enabler a commonplace.

Google used the cloud to create a further revolution in cash management on its search engine by letting app creators drive sales directly through their apps in real time without waiting for lengthy sales and cash conversion cycles. On Google, customers point, click, and close. Cash moves immediately across the cloud, cutting receivable days to zero and cutting inventory days in some supply chains from tens to single digits, thus freeing up valuable working capital, increasing cash velocity, and giving vendors balance sheet flexibility unknown before.

As much as apps are a creative force, app revenue flows can disintermediate whole industries. For example, since its inception after World War Two, to cover production costs, the TV business relied on large revenues paid before a TV season in "up fronts" from both advertisers and distributors like cable TV companies in the expectation of big audiences.

In the Apposphere, by contrast, these revenue streams run in reverse. There are no up fronts and, in the example of Netflix, TV networks must fund their own shows, now apps. To gain a return, they then must sell these apps one customer at a time and pay an app store like iTunes a commission for the privilege. This is like saying that the Mississippi will run north instead of south, emptying into the Gulf of St. Lawrence through the Great Lakes. All the beneficiaries of this change in flow will be different.

If apps are successful they may attract in-app advertising but only proportional to the precise number of hits they get on the app server. No more huge upfronts based on wild promises of millions of viewers that may be supported after the fact by vague and inaccurate telephone surveys. The app server knows precisely to the hit, where each came from, and when. Like Google, TV networks will get paid by the hit, no more and no less, and only when the hit comes. Many networks are so burdened by production costs— watch a TV show being made on the streets of New York and count the people involved—that they will not survive. Such is the power of the marginal cost revolution.

How powerful? To consumers, a TV, no matter how big, thin, or energy efficient, is simply an app enablement device that provides a window into an app store. This provides TV makers with long-term, low-risk revenue streams.

But, selling TVs, as Samsung does, that give customers access to Google's app store rather than its own, means giving up all the potential app revenue and foregoing all the customer Big Data needed to develop next gen products. This is a dead-end business model.

The day that Apple and Google make their app stores the easiest to access on a TV, the brands of the TV makers will vanish. For the Japanese consumer electronics sector, this is a mortal threat and one to which it has been largely blind. All because it did not have the Super Genba ability and cash velocity to identify and profit from the cloud membranes the way Konosuke's tap water philosophy said it should.

Because the cloud measures all apps and all app enablement devices in real time, the resulting Big Data is a huge new pool of customer metrics and ethnographic information that can be leveraged quickly into new and better offerings, even to create new demand ahead of competitors.

Just how valuable is the ethnographic information generated by Big Data? Konosuke walked the streets of Osaka questioning customers one-by-one on how they used his products and showing them better ways of using them. Markets soon got way too big for anyone to do this alone. For decades, companies tried to get the same information by questioning distributors, buying market research, or hiring mystery shoppers to understand in-store buying patterns. Compared to cloud-born Big Data like Google's, however, this is incomplete, expensive, indirect, and late.[39]

Apps generate ethnographic data that your competitors don't see, gaining you proprietary Super Genba advantages in creating new demand before your competitors know there is a market to be tapped. This is how the Super Genba customer information premium works: great insight combined with superior ethnography to create new, untapped demand that only you can serve—at a premium.

Today, whether you are a consumer, a business, or even a machine, by using the cloud your suppliers know far more

---

[39] What Google knows about you is astonishing. See Gara, Tom. "64,019 Searches: A Dark Journey Into My Google History." *WSJ Blogs - Corporate Intelligence*, July 31, 2013

about your usage patterns, quality problems, and future needs than before. Clouds turn companies into giant phased-array radars locked onto their customers anywhere in the world. The Big Data companies gather allows them to eliminate large amounts of cost while improving quality, in real time regardless of market or geography, something that was unthinkable before the cloud.

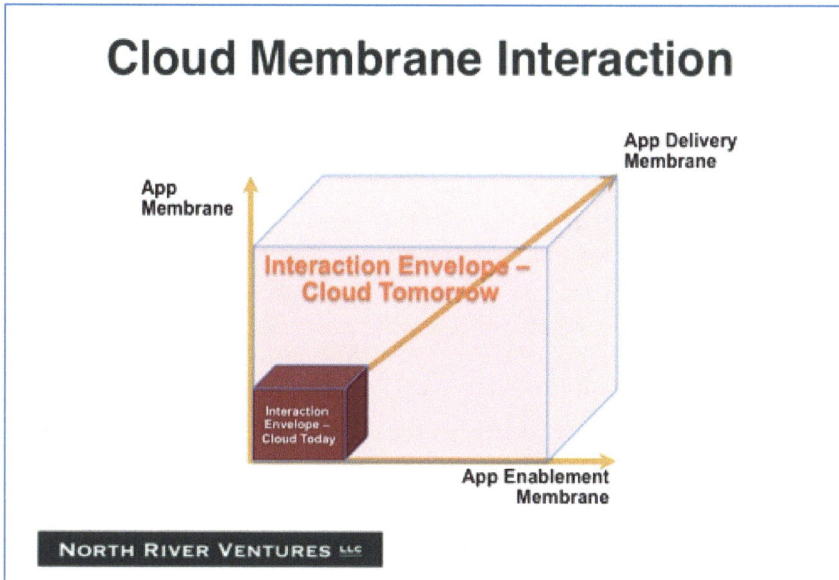

Cloud Membrane Interaction

App Delivery Membrane

App Membrane

Interaction Envelope – Cloud Tomorrow

Interaction Envelope – Cloud Today

App Enablement Membrane

NORTH RIVER VENTURES LLC

Not only can companies launch fewer and better-targeted products, but in the same process, cloud-born Big Data cuts the risk of product failure. While nothing can entirely eliminate failure, clouds sharply reduce the risk that products will launch straight off a cliff. Clouds make R&D more effective dollar-for-dollar.

Clouds also identify multiple revenue opportunities as their Big Data show the most profitable and enduring membrane interactions. As Apple found with iTunes and other services, cloud membrane interactions allow suppliers to turn one-time product sales into long-term annuity sale relationships that can last decades, reinforcing product sales, like iPhones and iMacs, while providing a smooth launchpad for unique new product categories like the iPad. The Cloud Revolution is a Super Genba sales revolution too.

We can make several observations about cloud membrane interactions:

1. Membranes always interact

2. There is no fixed interaction formula

3. Successful business models identify the most profitable interactions and get there first

Membrane interaction creates, as Apple was the first to find, the basis of a new generation of customer education systems and tools. If cloud companies are anything, they are giant universities, showing their customers how to use cloud tools grow and profit in ways that the customers never foresaw. On the cloud, this interactive relationship is reciprocal: Customers and producers teach each other in real time. Everyone has something to teach and everyone has something to learn. Doing this keeps customers, which is always cheaper than trying to gain new ones.

The better a device's ability to enable apps, therefore, the stronger its market position and the more likely it is to command a premium. Whatever allows app users more power, wins. This holds, no matter the device.

Also compelling is the fact that in the cloud world, products like my Skycaddie can be replaced, upgraded, or even rendered obsolete by more advanced products or entire systems, without the cloud itself being replaced. If anything, the data stream on the cloud that is mineable by producers just gets richer.

SUPER GENBA LESSONS

- Taken all together, the scale economics of the cloud have the effect, as Hartwig Rüll's work showed, of raising both:

- o OFCF/ R&D
- o OFCF/other SG&A

- The number of unnecessary products that never get launched in a Super Genba system cuts deeply into R&D and SG&A budgets. The Apposphere identifies what customers want and how they use what they want in real time. Nothing in this prevents mistakes, but their number is reduced and they are easier to recover from.
- The key is to identify the most profitable interactions between the Cloud Membranes and to get there first, as Apple did with iTunes. It really does not matter what your business is, because the cloud is so big and expanding so fast. What matters is that you have Super Genba-like ability to gain the most scalable opportunities before anyone else.

SUPER GENBA STEP TWO: DRIVE SALES

A quarter of a century ago, Sean White and I had just sold telecommunications market research publisher, Northern Business Information, to McGraw-Hill when NEC approached us looking for advice on how best to sell profitably.

NEC was trying to understand why its products were not selling well outside Japan, specifically in the U.S. We worked with NEC on this problem for two years and folded our advice into our first book, *Beating Japan* (Dutton, 1993), published as *nihon no jakuten* in Japan. *Super Genba* is the extension of that advice.

NEC was a pioneer in computerizing telecommunications systems and by rights today should be one of the leaders in building cloud-enabled networks, if not the leader. NEC has no such role today.

At the time we were seriously puzzled by NEC's problem. It came to us complaining that while its products were great in its estimation, its U.S. sales were poor. Our researchers at Northern Business Information had shown the sales failings of Japanese high tech companies for years. Time and again they saw that leading Japanese companies in our sector suffered falling market shares everywhere outside Japan no matter how well they did in Japan. Our staff noticed the same phenomenon in computers, software, and integrated circuits, especially processors. In other words, in all the drivers of the information revolution, Japan was not a player. Where it had once been a player, it was no longer.

This made no sense. These companies had lots of Japanese government support and had had this support since the end of WWII, then nearly half a century in the past. We often wondered if something systemic was wrong. But, not knowing much about Japan—we had never been there—we did not think much more on the subject.

Until, that is, NEC walked in the door and asked for a solution. Our answer came within only a few days and one or two telephone calls. NEC had no sales organization, no marketing function, no customer relationships, and no knowledge of what customers valued. This was hardly credible at the time and we were sure there must be more to NEC's ills than this. So we went to Japan to find out.

We soon discovered that our few minutes of phone calls had produced the correct answer. In Japan, we were shown factories, labs, and large Japanese sales, planning, and other organizations. There were even large numbers working on overseas sales. What these people were doing in Japan, we could not understand because they could do nothing there of any value. Sure enough, nowhere did anyone discuss overseas customers or show any knowledge of these customers, how they operated, and what their needs might be. There was no customer information at all.

What there was, and plenty of it, was a lot of information on Japan's top telecommunications carrier, NTT, then the largest company in the world by market capitalization. But NTT demanded systems that no one else in the world used or wanted and all the information NEC had about NTT was valueless elsewhere. Undaunted by this obvious problem, NEC had a second set of products for use outside Japan that increased costs enormously, but, oddly to our way of thinking, no information on those to whom it was to sell these products. While NEC had the advantage of being a pioneer in the computerization of telecommunications systems, and had had some early success with these products, it had not been able to turn this leadership into enduring, profitable sales.

The company owed all of its early success in North America to a single Japanese executive who had lived in the U.S., traveled all across the country selling the hard way like Konosuke, meeting customers, working with them to solve problems, and doing what good sales leaders should. But, he had been promoted, brought back to Japan, and sidelined for being too "American." Immediately, NEC's U.S. sales efforts foundered.

What we found was an endless stream of innovations flowing out of Japanese labs into foreign markets that had no use for these products. And an equally endless frustration in Japan with the performance of the tiny overseas sales teams that were supposed to shoehorn these unneeded innovations into their customers. The Japanese engineers blamed the sales people for not selling and the sales people blamed the Japanese engineers for not giving them vendible products. Customers did not factor into the discussion.

NEC's weak structure meant that in the U.S., NEC got only those sales people who could not make it working for the top competitors of the day. No one else was interested in working there. These under-performers simply increased the level of under-performance, driving headquarters nuts.

The most obvious weakness was that accountability was concentrated at the tiny sales front end of the NEC organization, but all the authority was concentrated far away from the field sales force in a complex mix of Japan-based staff and line groups that we could not figure out. After a lot of confusion, we had the bright idea of asking everyone casually over lunch or dinner which university they had attended when young. Back at our hotel we flagged all the Tokyo University graduates on the organization charts NEC gave us and redrew the lines of authority between the Todai grads. It worked perfectly. But how would a U.S. customer get this information? Why would it bother?

In my work with many Japanese companies over the quarter century since, I have seen countless failures like this: companies operating as if their overseas customers did not exist. I am often asked why Japan, the early leader in cell phones and cellular services—NTT DoCoMo had cloud-based app services long before anyone else—lost to Apple's iPhone.

The answer is as simple as it is obvious. Japanese companies do no ethnographic research in their target markets around the world. So they have no idea what customers want or how they use products and systems to advance their goals.

Making matters worse, Japanese consumer electronics makers, for example, usually insist on selling through distributors, guaranteeing that they get only the most limited information about their customers. There are direct sales outlets like Sony Style, but these are rare and unfocused. Apple stores, by contrast, are focused ethnography centers that happen to sell products. Apple relies on resellers for the bulk of its sales, just as Japanese companies do. But the stream of customer information that comes in from its own store and internet sales, combined with the volumes of customer information that hit its iCloud servers from a wide range of interfaces on Apple products, allows Apple to load its distributors with products that it knows in advance its customers want.

Apple is one of those giant, phased-array radars pointed at customers all over the world.

In our own company, Northern Business Information, we had run into the same problems as NEC, but a half-decade previously. Our biggest customer worldwide was AT&T, which routinely consumed everything we published. They used this information to make spending decisions in the many billions of dollars. Mistakes on our part could have a huge impact on AT&T's ability to generate shareholder value.

Sean and I began to notice problems with our AT&T relationship. There was a troubling trickle of complaints and we worried that orders from our best customer might fall off. If AT&T was unhappy, could the others—all, like NEC and NTT, the biggest companies in the global telecommunications sector—be far behind? If so, our business was at risk.

Our solution was simple and effective. I called AT&T and asked if we could meet at their head office in nearby New Jersey. I asked that they bring everyone who used our publications and every complaint about our company that they could think of. I brought several of our top product development people and, of course, the woman who led our AT&T sales efforts.

At that first meeting we were buried with AT&T's complaints. For some, our products were sometimes unusable. For others, important market data was not included. I asked each member of my product development team to respond on the spot. I didn't want us crawling back to our offices to compile answers for delivery to AT&T weeks hence.

My team solved about fifty percent of AT&T's issues at the meeting and we delivered these data within days. We could solve another forty percent with some changes on both our parts. From us, new information with better packaging to make it easier for AT&T to use. From AT&T, better ways to use our information when they got it. The last ten percent, we told them at our meeting, were requests for information that was not available by any known means. Since AT&T didn't know this, they were more than satisfied to find that there were things about the market that they could never quantify.

For me, the biggest revelation was this last ten percent. I had always thought that revealing the limitations of what we could do was showing customers our weakness, never a good thing. Instead, I learned that by telling customers in advance of the physical limits to our information gathering, we were eliminating a high risk unknown. Because AT&T was using our information to take billion dollar risks, knowing this was vital to them, cost us nothing, and gave us information about AT&T that no one else had. It had never occurred to me that telling customers something negative would be an enduring competitive advantage. These are things that, if you are not close to your customers, you will never know.

I arranged follow-on meetings quarterly and ensured direct lines of communication between the AT&T team and me and my team, making sure that our AT&T sales leader was in the mix rather than stuck with all the complaints and no way to solve them.

Soon, we got no complaints. Then, we began to get requests for information that we had never thought of providing. This gave us deeper insights into our customer's needs than our competition had.

We extended the program to all our top accounts. Then we added a killer innovation. We integrated our customers into our research by sending them computer disks (this was pre-Internet) with all our market data spreadsheets, showing our calculations, projections, and assumptions. They could then change these by inserting their own assumptions. This proved to be a huge competitive advantage because it went against industry wisdom that you should never give away your methods, only the results of these methods. Because no one else did this, we gained more customers, more business with the ones that we had, and tons more information about how to develop profitable new products when our customers called to discuss our methods.

Before long, we were crushing our competition with the data sets of such accuracy and prescience that most of our competitors left the market. We became the global reference standard for decision making in telecommunications, one of the biggest markets in the world.

When McGraw-Hill started looking around for an acquisition to fill a gap in its product line, its M&A team discovered that we were the gold standard. When they called our customers to ask about us, they got glowing reports, all of which we got to see after McGraw-Hill bought our company.

The result: an unsolicited offer from McGraw-Hill well above any price that we could have imagined.

And all based on our prototypical Super Genba system of putting more of our best people in front of more of our best customers more of the time. By putting all of our people into the Super Genba, we did what NEC did not do: We pushed authority and accountability into the customer interface.

Naturally, our prescription for NEC and in *Beating Japan* was: Design your company from the customer interface back into R&D rather than from R&D forward into customers. Make sure that you have more customer interaction in more parts of your ecosystem and learn how to turn that information into cash faster than others can. This was the beginning of the Super Genba system.

Had our uncomplicated recommendation been used by NEC—it wasn't—huge amounts of cost would have been cut as it eliminated useless R&D and simplified other SG&A systems. Operating earnings would have risen as value was added in the way that customers wanted and needed. Better still, NEC would have identified large, profitable markets long before its competition got there. Much of Japanese industry would have learned from this, there would have been no lost generation, and I would not be writing this book.

USE SUPER GENBA TO GET *KIZUNA* WITH CUSTOMERS

The story of how I decided to use the Japanese word *kizuna* to describe the goal of Super Genba is interesting. One evening, I was sitting with friends at the bar at *kizuna*, a sushi place in Osaka's Kyobashi district. I asked *taisho* what the word meant. He is a young guy and explained that he wanted to open his own restaurant but at his age he did not have the resources to do so. Then his friends, family, and suppliers got together and helped him launch his restaurant. In their honor he called it *kizuna* meaning the family-like bond it took to pull everything together.

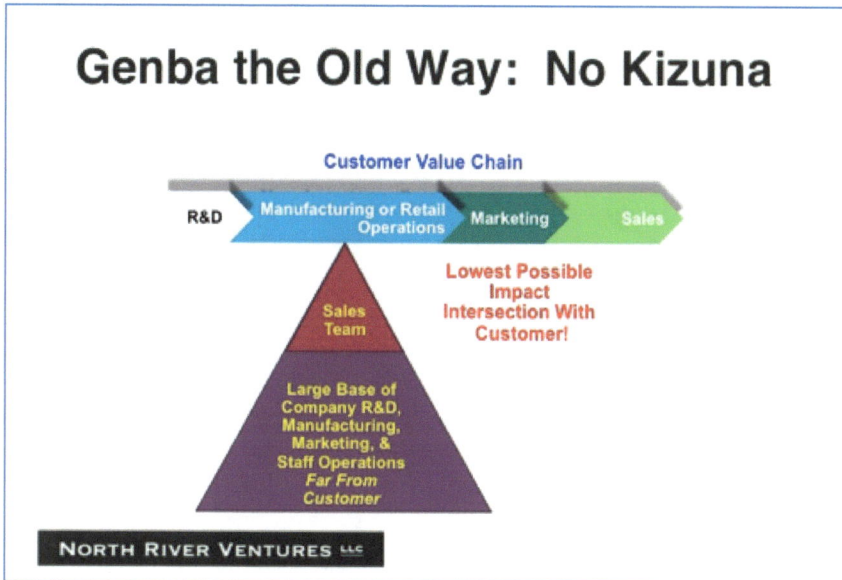

Genba the Old Way: No Kizuna

Customer Value Chain

R&D | Manufacturing or Retail Operations | Marketing | Sales

Lowest Possible Impact Intersection With Customer!

Sales Team

Large Base of Company R&D, Manufacturing, Marketing, & Staff Operations Far From Customer

NORTH RIVER VENTURES LLC

As soon as he said this I knew I had the word I needed to explain to the Japanese in their language what Super Genba is meant to do. It is an organization overlaid with a set of processes designed to create the *kizuna* between you and your customers that turns customer information into cash fast.

In old-fashioned *genba,* only sales people talk to customers. And only to customer purchasing organizations. Companies got:

- Minimal feedback
- The lowest level of sales contact
- Accountability separated from authority
- Minimum responsiveness to customers

With so many limitations, you must discount your way to market share, not a formula for scalable profitability.

This chart shows a B2B *genba* sales system. Product development starts with R&D in Japan. It works out from there, often over years, to a customer who could be in any industry, anywhere in the world, but always far removed from Japan-based product developers. This minimizes the customer information needed to turn customer information into cash quickly. There is no *kizuna* sales-doubling potential here.

The process is slow and usually means getting products to market that are either too late or maladapted or both. Simple physics says that as customer information begins its flow from sales step-by-step through all the parts of a supplier organization to R&D, parts of this information, and its speed, are lost at each step. And more is lost as it flows back. Because the sales intersection has the lowest possible impact with the customer, what information the company gets in the first place is limited. What finally ends up back with the customer is valueless. As a result, market share erodes in many markets simultaneously. Some customers outside Japan are not developed at all.

Customers see only sales people. But sales teams have the least to do with product development and the least influence on their companies. Their sales contacts are often at the lowest possible level in customer accounts, a place where selling on price is key. Premium positioning is almost unknown. This is what had happened to NEC and very nearly happened to Sean and me.

High sales risks are baked into this process: Most company personnel never see a customer and those who do see customers see people at too low a level to affect outcomes. Customer information deficits are built into the business model.

In Super Genba, by contrast, the *genba* is so big that everyone, regardless of function or seniority, works with customers daily to generate more action in more places, creating *kizuna*. Companies get:

- The three mores—more of our best people talking to more of our best customers more of the time

- Accountability and authority integrated everywhere in the organization for:

    - Maximum responsiveness

    - Maximum customer information

    - Premium customers

    - Premium pricing

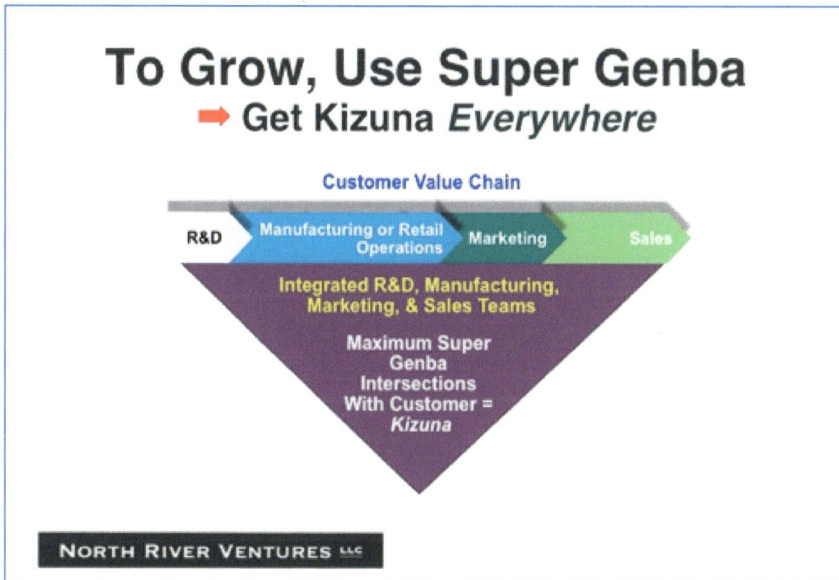

To scale to 2X sales and 3X profits, companies need this type of everything-on-the-surface, everywhere and all at once, Super Genba structure designed to get customer information fast and turn this into cash fast. As in this chart, everyone sells. All employees, all functions including HQ, all levels, all business units, all geographies—integrate with all customer operations, creating *kizuna*.

Kizuna feedback drives R&D directly, reduces the risk of product failure, and raises OFCF/R&D ratios. *Kizuna* cross-operational integration locks customers into a service relationship first, as Sean White and I discovered firsthand with AT&T, and a product relationship second. This service-first relationship is what was missing at NEC.

In *The Game Changer*, A.G. Lafley, the CEO of Procter and Gamble, and his co-author Ram Charan, call this structure the "inverted pyramid," (above) in which the resource base of the company is in constant customer contact everywhere, worldwide. This, they say, creates "a flow of communication and planning between the functions of each company—expert to expert, speaking a common language with joint goals and measures."[40] This massively reduces sales risks and increases the flow of customer information to where it has most effect.

Lafley and Charan echo what Sean White and I discovered in the 1980s, that weak sales organizations intersect with customers at the weakest point where the resources of both are minimal. It is the job of this weak link to put the value of the whole company before its customers. This, Lafley and Charan say, is mathematically impossible; there are just too many moving parts in your and your customers' organizations. Lafley and Charan's solution, like ours, is to get the broad base of the pyramid across all functions from R&D to sales locked onto important customers in a synchronized way. In modern business, they say, "knowledge sharing is the big scale driver when we have

---

[40] A.G. Lafley and Ram Charan, *The Game Changer: How You Can Drive Revenue and Profit Growth With Innovation* (New York: Random House, 2008) p. 140

done it right."[41] That means both within your company and between it and its customers.

By putting more of our best people in front of more of our best customers more of the time, *kizuna*:

- Better meets the needs of our customers
- Takes costs out of both our and our customers' supply chains
- Increases our prosperity and that of our customers

Properly done and automated, Lafley and Charan famously say, "The orders write themselves."

SUPER GENBA AND THE LANGUAGE OF CASH VELOCITY

Lafley and Charan's system, just like the one Sean and I developed nearly thirty years ago, is designed to get customer information and turn this into cash quickly. But there is another aspect to Super Genba sales that is essential to success, especially in B2B sales.

It is learning to speak the common language of cash velocity. You can see from the chart that in B2B markets all the key drivers of my Cash Velocity Index are common to all customer managers at all levels of seniority and in all functions and geographies. Equally, cash velocity supports the customer's balance sheet and income statement at the same time. In other words, if you teach your customers how your products and services improve their Cash Velocity Indices, your sales approach will work as well in their boardrooms as on their factory floors. This is where Lafley and Charan's shared knowledge earns huge dividends, as Nitto Denko discovered by integrating its manufacturing processes into its products in its customers' factories.

---

[41] Ibid. p. 99.

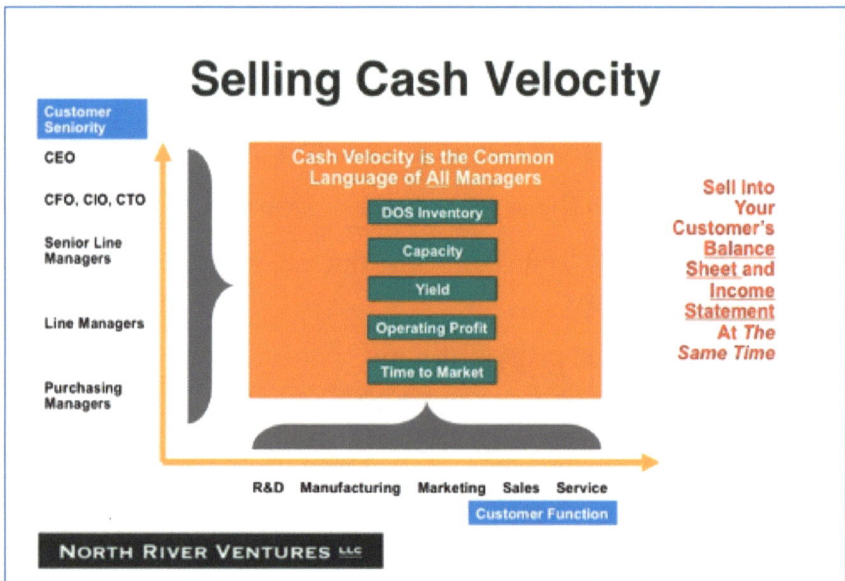

Selling Cash Velocity

Customer Seniority

CEO

CFO, CIO, CTO

Senior Line Managers

Line Managers

Purchasing Managers

Cash Velocity is the Common Language of All Managers

DOS Inventory

Capacity

Yield

Operating Profit

Time to Market

Sell Into Your Customer's Balance Sheet and Income Statement At *The Same Time*

R&D   Manufacturing   Marketing   Sales   Service

Customer Function

NORTH RIVER VENTURES LLC

Speaking in the language of cash velocity—everything you sell must measurably improve customer Cash Velocity Indices—allows you to do what is most important for your customers and to keep doing it. Just as we did with AT&T, speaking a common language brings in information on customer operating challenges that no one else has, a major competitive advantage.

I cannot tell you the number of times that I sit in meetings with teams that cannot speak cash velocity and that have just been stunned as a result by a customer rejection that they never saw coming. Often, these teams have only the lowest-level contacts in customers, a level where the *lingua franca* is the least valuable information, price. Rarely are these teams integrated with full support from their own R&D and manufacturing operations. I recently had to remove an $80 billion a year in sales Japanese company from multibillion-dollar a year initiative because of this.

If you speak cash velocity, you get insights into where you can integrate your operations with customers and improve the cash velocity of both parties.

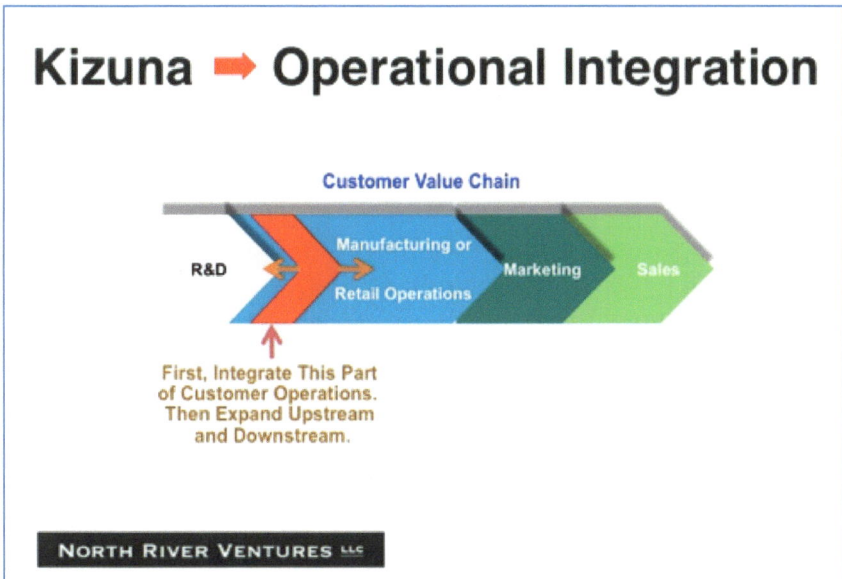

Kizuna ➡ Operational Integration

Customer Value Chain

R&D — Manufacturing or Retail Operations — Marketing — Sales

First, Integrate This Part of Customer Operations. Then Expand Upstream and Downstream.

NORTH RIVER VENTURES LLC

Using this chart, Nitto Denko famously turned a 140-day receivable cycle with a top customer into a 15-day cycle with a newer one. Soon, the second, profitable customer displaced the first in sales value and the company used its system to add other profitable customers. Not a moment too soon because the 140-day customer ran into deep financial problems and Nitto avoided a huge risk to its balance sheet.

Quite apart from the simple question, would you rather get paid in 15 days or 140, there is another, more profound question. Would you rather be in the high-risk business of selling commodities with 140-day terms or in the much lower-risk business of selling cash with 15-day terms? This is why, I tell CEOs, you must make sure that your Super Genba teams know how to sell cash to your customers. Those who sell cash are almost impossible to displace because they drive customer financials directly and are as valuable to the customer's CEO as they are to its purchasing department. Fail to sell cash and you can be displaced by anyone with a cheaper product.

USE SUPER GENBA TO EXPLOIT THE CLOUD-ENABLED CASH PHASE SHIFT

Since the invention of double entry accounting by the Genoese in 1340 and its codification by Luca Pacioli a century and half later, businesses have focused on cost at the top line (what they buy) and bottom line (how they manage). Cash velocity was a result of these efforts. Early banking tools like letters of credit and factoring were designed to ease the working capital management problems inherent in the system.

Cloud computing changes all the assumptions of seven centuries of business operations. By their nature, clouds allow instant communication with any customer or any supplier anywhere in a company's ecosystem. Information from one can be transmitted seamlessly to the other in real time. Businesses can identify and eliminate cash wait states anywhere in their systems, often in fractions of a second.

Using the cloud, companies can restructure themselves in fundamental ways. The cloud is the glue that holds the company together and bonds it to its customers and to its supply chain. Clouds allow companies to integrate their operations with those of their customers.

The most famous proto cloud example is Proctor and Gamble's satellite network-based integration of its Pampers production line with Walmart's cash registers.[42] The moment a box of Pampers goes through Walmart's checkout, P&G's production line begins to pump out a replacement box. This gives both P&G and Walmart more sales for less inventory and less of every resource needed to move unneeded products to stores like oil, gas, and trucks. With the cloud, small companies can do the same thing.

---

[42] *Walmart and the Falling Information Cost Curve*, North River Ventures LLC, February 1995

Clouds make it easy for a modern business to think of cash is its primary driver, as Apple does, and of cost as the result of cash-driven actions.

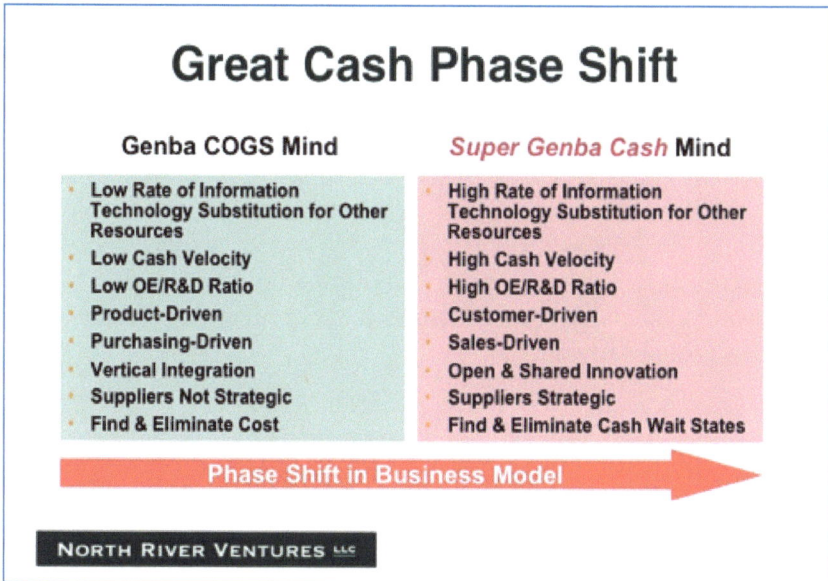

Great Cash Phase Shift

Genba COGS Mind	Super Genba Cash Mind
• Low Rate of Information Technology Substitution for Other Resources	• High Rate of Information Technology Substitution for Other Resources
• Low Cash Velocity	• High Cash Velocity
• Low OE/R&D Ratio	• High OE/R&D Ratio
• Product-Driven	• Customer-Driven
• Purchasing-Driven	• Sales-Driven
• Vertical Integration	• Open & Shared Innovation
• Suppliers Not Strategic	• Suppliers Strategic
• Find & Eliminate Cost	• Find & Eliminate Cash Wait States

Phase Shift in Business Model →

NORTH RIVER VENTURES LLC

I call this The Great Cash Phase Shift and you can see its wide-ranging impact on this chart.

The thinking of companies on either side of this chart—McLuhan's "frontier between two cultures"—is profoundly different. Companies on the left focus on cost and put everything else at a lower level of importance. Critically, they think of information technology, so important for shortening up cash wait states to the cash-minded companies, as a cost to be minimized. Companies on the right, by contrast, focus on anything that turns customer information into cash fast. This is McLuhan's frontier expressed in how companies manage their balance sheet and profit-and-loss results.

As I said in the Introduction, I have often proposed to Japanese firms that they save money on travel expense and connect to customers globally in real time to solve problems by putting in a Cisco-type telepresence video conference system. A quick calculation shows that even the most expensive versions will pay for themselves in about three months. The answer I usually get is that we are cutting IT budgets, we don't have enough bandwidth in our network for telepresence systems, and have no plans to change. Indeed, as I mentioned in the Introduction, it is usually impossible to send standard size files—a .pdf file of this book is a good example—to Japanese companies because their servers choke. This response means that solving customer problems quickly is the lowest priority, not the highest. Then, when sales go wrong, some poor salesman at the *genba*, who has no influence over company decision-making, gets blamed.

From this one mistep flow all the others. In cost-driven companies, cash velocity is low, working capital loads are high, and suppliers are forced to provide banking services by accepting over-long payment terms. Forcing suppliers to be bankers weakens them, making the whole ecosystem a diminished force in the market.

In Japan, the larger the cost-driven company, the more marked the tendency to favor vertical integration. The Panasonic that Kirk Nakamura took over was an example. These companies think vertical integration gives them more control over costs even though it builds in huge cash wait states. Similarly, these firms favor centralized R&D and avoid outsourcing or shared innovation.

As I said before, Japanese managers often complain to me that by the time they get to market it is too late, or that R&D and product proliferation strategies designed to derisk poor time-to-market don't work. If these managers switched their orientation to cash velocity, most of their problems would have obvious solutions.

When you look at cash-driven companies like Walmart, the reasons become clear. As the P&G story showed, Walmart was the first company of any size to use IT to eliminate the wait states of cash in its ecosystem. In the sixteen years after it did this, it grew four and a half times and suffered only the smallest ripples from any of the recessions during this period, especially the 2008 Crash.

If you look at one of Walmart's biggest competitors, German retailer Metro, which is cost-driven, you will see a different result. Sales for 2011 were 2% below 2008 and profits 60% lower. In the comparable period Walmart sales were up 17% and profits up 7%. Just before the 2008 crash, I brought up this point with Metro's CFO. He told me that if he tried to run his company like Walmart, it would be bankrupt. This was perhaps one of the most foolish and illogical comments I have ever heard from a senior officer of a company. He was asked to leave the firm not long afterward.

In a parallel with the European Reformation that followed the Gutenberg press, today we have cloud-driven, cash-oriented companies like Apple—the reformed—competing head-to-head with unclouded, cost-driven competitors—the unreformed—many of whom are Japanese. The two do not understand each other's premises. Even though anyone can read what Apple does in its annual report and then do the same thing Apple does, no one in Japan's CE sector has. The result is sequential corporate failure.

It is axiomatic, in addition, that cash touch points are customer information touch points. Get information on all the cash touch points in your ecosystem and you get large amounts of information on customers and their role in your ecosystem. COGS-driven companies don't get this information.

You can see here what this means: a bifurcation of customers between the COGS-oriented and the cash velocity-oriented. I have a great example. When Nitto Denko launched its Global Account Management program, I expected that we would quickly see differences between Nitto's COGS-minded customers and its cash velocity-minded customers. We did, of course, but the details were quite impressive.

Nitto had two customers, one European the other American, that competed head-to-head in a fast growing market. The European customer was COGS-driven, had the highest market share, but almost none of the profits. The American firm was cash velocity-driven, had a small market share but the bulk of the profits in the sector.

Super Genba Selling

- **High Cash Velocity**
  - **Low DOS Inventory**
  - **Low DOS AR**
  - **High/Low DOS AP**
- **High OE/R&D, SG&A Ratios**
- **Short Time-to-Market**
- **Short R&D Recovery**
- **Open & Shared Innovation**
- **Process Driven**
- **Suppliers Strategic**
- **Mission: Find Cash**

Wide Sales Focus: We MUST Sell into ALL of These Customer Needs!!

NORTH RIVER VENTURES LLC

Nitto's GAM teams saw that the two had radically different structures that demanded very different sales approaches. The European customer had a range of products, each with its own supply chain and design operations. Some of its products used more outsourcing than others. This customer did not have a single design or sourcing philosophy. The American customer had a single product, sourcing, and design philosophy optimized to minimize cash wait states in its ecosystem and add value at well-defined points.

We could see that the poor profits of the European customer were the result of its chaotic operations and that the company was operating with a large customer information deficit. Even though it was a market dominator, this could not last, and while Nitto's sales potential appeared good, increasing sales to this customer brought with it increasing risks that the customer's market position might collapse. Quickly.

You cannot use Super Genba on such a customer because it has no matching operations into which to plug the *kizuna* inverted pyramid. You have to sell the old-fashioned way, which means selling on price. *Super Genba* logic says that you must carefully derisk these customers. Never rely too much on them just because they are big.

By contrast, the American customer operated under Super Genba rules that made its future uncommonly bright. By identifying its cash velocity drivers and meeting its design and sourcing requirements, Nitto did very well. Naturally, Nitto focused on this customer, treated it as a growth opportunity, and the results were favorable.

Soon, Nitto's European customer ran into the trouble that its Cash Velocity Index said that it would. Forewarned, Nitto was able to manage the downside.

SUPER GENBA LESSONS

- Super Genba Future Creators have a language of their own. They communicate across a broad front and have a wide range of *kizuna* bonding opportunities.
- The reverse is not true, however. It is impossible for a COGS-oriented company to see into the future across McLuhan's frontier and understand how cash velocity helps it grow profitably.
- In Super Genba cash velocity-driven companies, you have to sell process simplification that shortens cash wait states, thus improving both customer balance sheets and income statements and your own. This involves your CEO and CFO, both of whom will be

directly involved. Now, ask yourself if your sales team knows how to sell cash velocity, let alone manage C-level relationships. Really well-trained sales teams know how to do this.

SUPER GENBA STEP THREE: MANAGE INNOVATION

We have seen that the inverted pyramid of the Super Genba *kizuna* structure floods a company with customer information across all its functions, geographies, and levels of management. Super Genba innovation management turns this customer information into value faster than the competition.

To do this, R&D must:

- Be decentralized to customers
- Focus only on what adds value to those customers
- Outsource, open source, or crowd source the rest

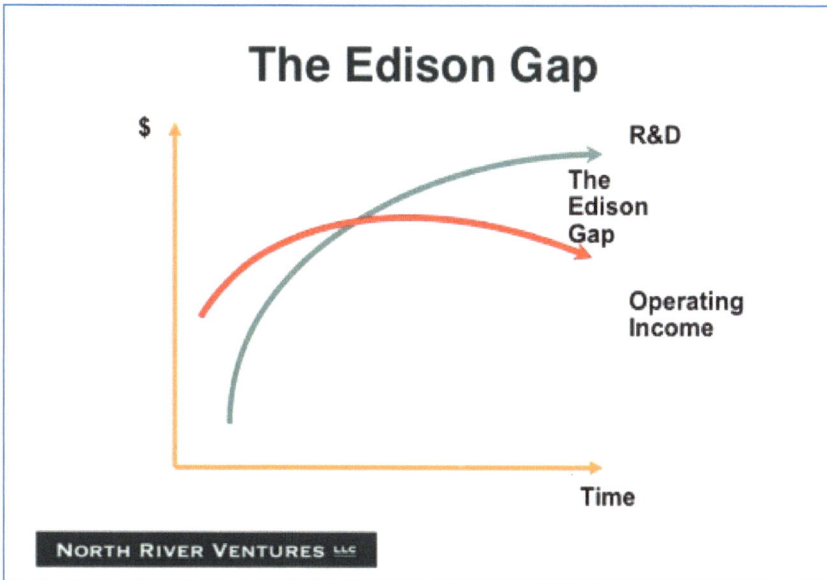

The Edison Gap

NORTH RIVER VENTURES LLC

Traditional, centralized R&D doesn't work well in a world where customer information and time dominate. Nor does R&D designed to promote vertically integrated systems work well because vertical integration increases the Hubble Effect. As a result, this R&D is focused on internal agendas and is too rigid to flex with the speed of the market.

You can see the problems of doing R&D the old fashioned way with the Edison Gap that, at the Corporate Innovation Project, we named after Thomas Edison, the father of corporate labs. The Edison Gap opens when centralized R&D stops scaling and R&D expense outruns operating earnings.

The Gap has had an impact on many Japanese companies for decades. Some have not recovered their R&D for thirty years yet keep pouring money into an R&D hole in the ground, on the assumption that people will magically buy. Unless, of course, they don't. For these firms, every yen that they spend on R&D loses money. This makes no sense.

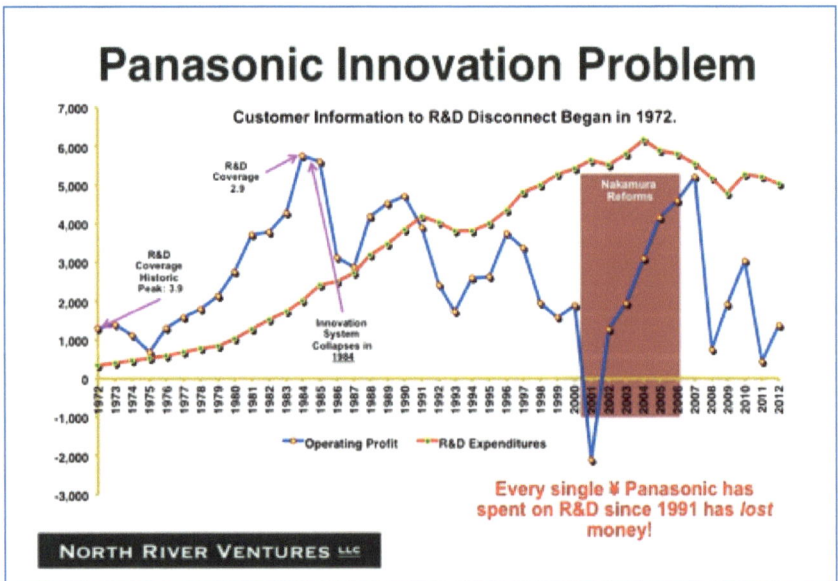

It doubly makes no sense because of the amount of other SG&A that must also be poured into selling products that no one wants.

Typical is Panasonic, a company that had a healthy operating earnings-to-R&D of nearly 4.0 in 1972. This ratio declined year after year and was less than 1.0 by the mid-eighties, at which point Panasonic fell into the Edison Gap and stopped making money on its R&D. No one seemed to notice until Kirk Nakamura's vigorous reform efforts in the 2001-2006 period pushed it back to nearly to 1.0. But the ratio collapsed again after he retired. Panasonic's innovation engine died 40 years ago and the firm, though many times its 1972 size, now trades for only a few months worth of sales.

These data—which you can see repeated in many firms in Japan and elsewhere—beg the question. Seeing such a chart, why would a company keep pushing out new products into new markets without asking fundamental questions about its system? For such data to endure three decades until a CEO points to it and acts, is hard to fathom. And, once he retires, for it to fall back on old practices in spite of what its own data tells it, is still harder to fathom.

There can be only one logical reason: The system does not let enough people see their customers because the *genba* is too small. Innovation is done in the dark. My hard rule is that if you try to reenergize top line growth before Super Genba restructuring, shareholder value will decline relatively and may even decline absolutely. This is what happened to Panasonic.

Sure enough, there is a remarkable correlation between companies in the Edison Gap and low management grades driven by low Cash Velocity Indices. You will find that not all low management grade companies are in the Edison Gap. But you will find the reverse, that all Edison Gap companies have low management grades and poor Cash Velocity Indices.[43]

I advise supersizing the *genba* and attaching every R&D person to a customer account and insisting that they meet with their assigned customer as part of a Super Genba *kizuna* team at least quarterly, just as I did at my own company.

---

[43] *Closing the Edison Gap*, North River Ventures LLC, October 19, 2007

The benefits of doing this are immediate and extraordinary. Labs people are intelligent, and putting this intelligence in the customer interface creates value immediately. Nitto Denko's very first Super Genba Global Account Management meeting was in Europe. R&D members produced profitable results instantly. They told the team that they already had the solution to a seemingly intractable customer problem, a solution the field sales force knew nothing about. To repeat what Lafley and Charan say, "knowledge sharing is the big scale driver when we have done it right." Here we had an excellent example. It was instant and cost Nitto nothing.

With Super Genba, once-closed information channels open and innovation becomes useful and immediate. The best thing about this is not just that Super Genba knowledge sharing costs nothing but that it reduces R&D loads. It makes the P&L stronger just by changing the direction of internal and customer communications.

Because Super Genba puts R&D and manufacturing operations into the *genba*, side-by-side with sales staff, R&D gets high value customer information in real time. This focuses R&D on both customer needs and manufacturability and sharply reduces the risk of innovation failure. *Kizuna* provides early proprietary insight—things about customers that no one else sees—allowing you to gain large advantages, offering profitable products that stay profitable for longer than those of the competition.

In another great Nitto example, the company had gone to a lot of trouble to create technology centers for its customers. But these acted more like showrooms than active centers for solving real customer problems. By altering only slightly from showing Nitto products, a passive exercise, to helping customers simplify their business processes with Nitto solutions, an active exercise, the company gains large amounts of hard-to-get customer information at no additional cost. And is able to turn this information into meaningful innovation quickly.

Super Genba innovation is often process innovation in which close knowledge of customers allows a company to integrate itself with customers in ways that others cannot. iCloud is a process, not a product, and the iCloud customer interface is vital to Apple's ability to gain customers, keep them for very long periods, and extract enormous amounts of information to which competitors do not have access. This in turn becomes its innovation growth and profit engine.

Similarly, a manufacturer like P&G that can integrate its systems into those of its customers like Walmart offers process innovation, not product innovation. I tell innovation teams that if their products and processes can cut days of sales in inventory or receivables for their customers, they will be very hard to displace even by a superior or cheaper technology. Why? Because by improving your customer's balance sheet and profit-and-loss statement at the same time, you will get the attention of top management and keep it. Your innovations will always be welcome and your customers will suggest even more valuable ones as AT&T did for us.

Logically, however, if you are not in the Performance Zone, your *genba* is so small that the most you can expect from technology investment and innovation is to stay even. Usually, these investments destroy value.

The corollary of this is that to add value from technology investments and acquisitions, you must be in the Super Genba Performance Zone first. If you are not in The Zone, your investment priority must be business process innovation in your own company, not unfocused technology innovation for your customers. In other words, put the horse in front of the cart.

This brings up another point that Lafley and Charan make. You must see innovation as a whole company phenomenon.

They include ecosystem-wide innovations in distribution, supply chain, and human resource management as well, of course, in products and technologies. The whole system must support a culture of innovation and 50% of it must be outsourced to ensure optimal use of company resources in a timely fashion. I have found things as simple as a clever spreadsheet hidden from company-wide view in a factory in Thailand that revolutionized a company's view of itself and its customers.

You need to invest in technology, of course. But, if you have less than Grade A management, you must invest in business process innovation first to make these investments pay off.

I remember a sorry conversation with an executive at a Japanese high tech company with whom I had done business for thirty years. The executive said that nothing could be done to boost U.S. sales or make the U.S. division profitable until Japan sent new products. The idea that the business model had to be transformed before new technology could help profits was impossible to grasp. This company had put the cart before the horse for its entire history. No amount of product or technology can make up for poor process innovation.

The same is true for technology innovation. We have seen how Apple uses its top grade Super Genba Cash Velocity Indices to turn innovation into value, and how hard it is for companies with poor Cash and Capital Velocity Indices to make any kind of top line initiative accretive. In other words: an iPod anywhere else would have gone over like a lead balloon. At Apple, it lead to a decade-long string of hit products that is still unfolding.

Given the data we've seen in earlier chapters, a Sharp, Sony, or Panasonic could have launched an iPod but the product almost certainly would have failed for lack of broader business process innovation.

If low-grade companies put Super Genba business process innovation first, their technology innovations will pay off. If they do the reverse, all the technology innovations in Silicon Valley will not keep the wolf from the door. By contrast, high-grade Performance Zone companies already have the Super Genba business processes to make innovation accretive almost immediately and almost every time. And, when Super Genba company innovations fail, the downside risk to them is much smaller than for low-grade competitors.

This scary conclusion is a corollary of my Super Genba innovation management rule: No amount of technology innovation will add value for firms outside the Super Genba Performance Zone. It may actually destroy value.

Dead Zone companies have no choice but to shoot in the dark. Maybe they are right, maybe they are wrong. The point is, they have no way of knowing which. And they must literally flame off R&D and other SG&A to see their way in the dark. This costs everybody, especially shareholders.

Because of their superior customer knowledge, high Cash Velocity Index companies better manage their customers' experience of their products. I had dinner recently with a retired IBM account executive hired back on contract. He was thoroughly enjoying his new work for its complete lack of distraction. He told me that he was assigned to only one client, a major bank, and that he spent his days figuring out how to make that bank's services easier and better for its customers to use. Does your sales team do this?

IBM gets my A Grade and this example shows the benefit it derives: Customers drive its products and services in real time. The savings to IBM in R&D and projects that are never launched must be phenomenal. And the profits from those that are right on target make shareholders happy every day.

THE INNOVATION PERFORMANCE ENVELOPE

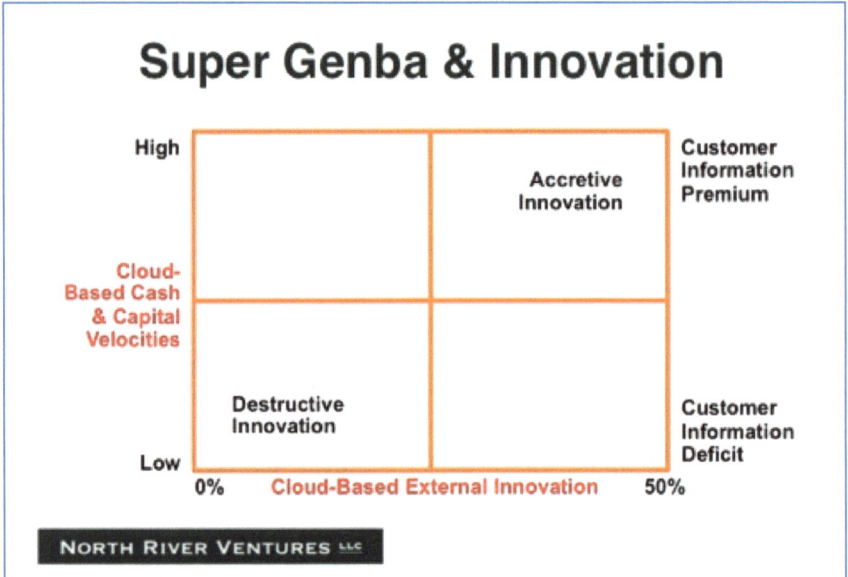

Super Genba & Innovation

High		Customer Information Premium
	Accretive Innovation	
Cloud-Based Cash & Capital Velocities		
	Destructive Innovation	Customer Information Deficit
Low		
0%	Cloud-Based External Innovation	50%

NORTH RIVER VENTURES LLC

In October 2004, I published my first analysis of the relationship between the Cash Velocity Index and innovation.[44] This was prompted by the comment of a consumer electronics industry executive that Samsung could out-innovate Sony at any time. My response was that Samsung also had a higher Cash Velocity Index than Sony at the time and a superior CVI drives superior innovation management rather than the other way around. I concluded that, because getting a top grade Cash Velocity Index means control of the sales process, it is vital to successful innovation. If you were to rebuild Sony, Sharp, or Panasonic, this is where you would have to start. The rest is secondary. In fact tertiary.

In this chart, you see why. I combined Lafley and Charan's 50% rule for outsourcing innovation with my rule on Cash and Capital Velocity Indices. What results explains why so

---

[44] *Apple* North River Ventures LLC, October 29, 2004

many Japanese companies have failed to innovate successfully. Many are in the bottom left corner where they have low Cash and Capital Velocity Indices, and therefore very little customer information, and thus an excessive reliance on internal innovation. The result, as happened at Panasonic, is destructive innovation, innovation that actually destroys value. You can see how innovation by itself cannot generate value except by accident. This is why so many Japanese companies have not recovered their R&D for decades.

Dead Zone companies cannot solve the two main innovation problems of customer information and time. If, for example, you were to examine Apple's innovation broadly, as A.G. Lafley would do, you would see something like the next chart.

Apple outsources as much as possible in all aspects of its business system, as in the chart, focusing on a thin fabric of proprietary hardware, software, and services that it can leverage in a variety of ways. As an example, people commonly talk of Apple's OSX operating system as if it is proprietary to Apple in the same way as Windows 8 is to Microsoft. In fact, OSX is built on Bell Labs' venerable and robust UNIX system. Apple makes the user interface to ensure that its customers get an Apple experience. But the core innovation was outsourced and derisked from its inception. Apple got to cut risk and time-to-market to fractions of what it would have been had it developed its own system from scratch.

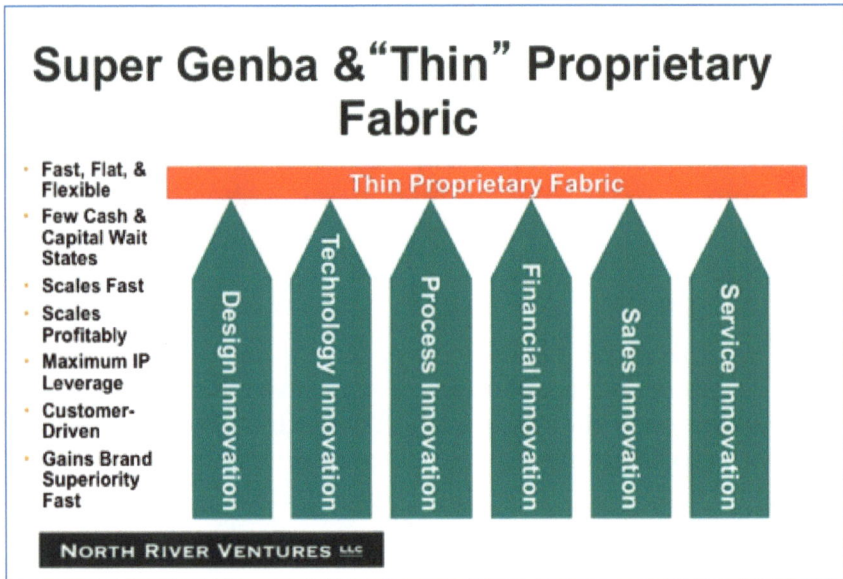

Super Genba &"Thin" Proprietary Fabric

- Fast, Flat, & Flexible
- Few Cash & Capital Wait States
- Scales Fast
- Scales Profitably
- Maximum IP Leverage
- Customer-Driven
- Gains Brand Superiority Fast

Thin Proprietary Fabric

Design Innovation · Technology Innovation · Process Innovation · Financial Innovation · Sales Innovation · Service Innovation

NORTH RIVER VENTURES LLC

This is the fundamental discipline that all R&D operations must have. Management must know what to insource and what to outsource for maximum effectiveness and shortest time-to-market.

MANAGING SUPER GENBA R&D

Managing R&D means carefully integrating customers, business models, and exit options into R&D from the beginning of each project as in the following chart. If you do this properly you can educate your customers on how they can best advance their own interests without actually using the words "customer education." The system does this by itself.

As in the chart, there are several steps in the process:

1. Source projects widely—everyone from customers to seemingly crazy ideas that someone in the company has.

2. Make sure that all projects are consistent with company strategy.

3. Initiate only projects that have the potential to double sales. Anything smaller is not serious.

4. Integrate customers at the earliest possible opportunity.

5. Ensure that from the beginning, each new project has a business case showing how sales can be doubled profitably. The R&D team must be responsible for this.

6. Make sure that each business case has a clearly defined exit option so that if it must be shut down, you know how to maximize values.

7. Ensure that R&D teams update and expand their business cases and exit options quarterly.

8. Have top management review each project and its business case quarterly.

9. If either the R&D case or the business case fails the review, exit promptly.

10. For each dropped project, go back to step one.

11. Know when to hand off projects to the business unit and have a well-defined process for doing this and the managers in place for doing it.

Too often I see very loosely managed R&D that has no sales doubling potential, no customer input, and just sort of floats along. I also see fear of failure. But failure is good—it's how we learn—so build it into the system. You should teach your R&D teams that there is value in everything that they do and show them how you plan to leverage that value no matter the outcome of the project. An R&D system with no failures is one that is operating well below optimal levels.

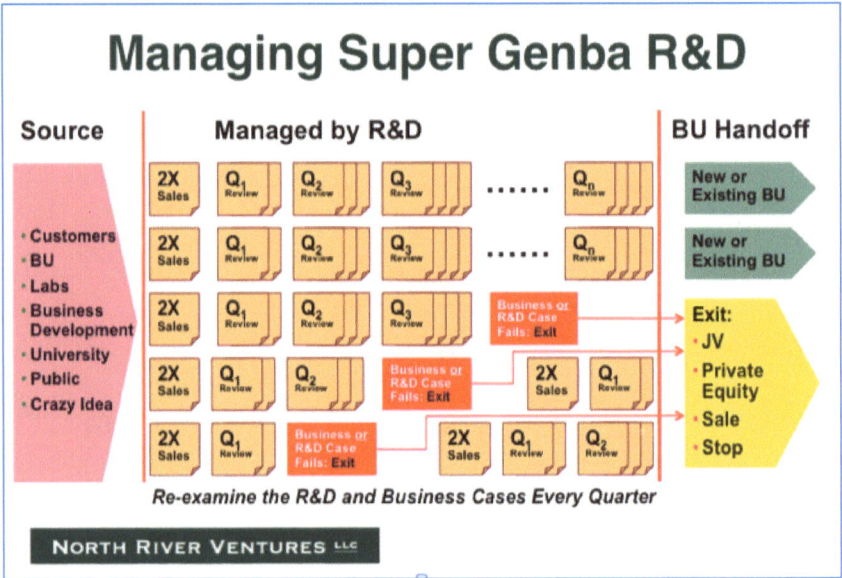

Managing Super Genba R&D

Source	Managed by R&D							BU Handoff

Re-examine the R&D and Business Cases Every Quarter

NORTH RIVER VENTURES LLC

For a company to take advantage of its Super Genba structure it must have a well-defined set of management processes that do not disturb the creative core of research operations. This is a balance that must be carefully managed. One of the best governors of this balance is customer input. Wherever possible, build R&D into customer operations as early as possible, thereby making customers the center of R&D initiatives. When we did this with AT&T, the benefits to us were immediate and enduring. Clients often tell me that they are afraid of revealing too much intellectual property too early to customers. This doesn't make a lot of sense. We do R&D to add value for customers, not to hide it from them. The sooner we begin to add that value, the better.

In one case, an R&D executive showed me that projects could spend as much time in market preparation as they did in the labs, delaying time to cash by as long as six years. My advice was to get customers in earlier and cut out this costly wait period.

SUPER GENBA LESSONS

1. The simplest way to identify innovation priorities is to have cash wait states short enough that labs are primed with high-quality, proprietary customer information in real time.

2. What makes low cash wait state winners so powerful in their markets is that they field a "thin" proprietary fabric that they leverage with a wide range of process innovations across all business functions from product design to sales and service.

3. High cash velocity companies get higher OFCF/R&D and higher OFCF/SG&A ratios than the competition. They can launch and sell new products and services profitably, a powerful twin advantage others don't have.

4. The sooner you integrate customers into your innovations, the better.

SUPER GENBA STEP FOUR: MANAGE MANUFACTURING

Once your *genba* has been supersized, the huge inflow of customer information will force you to allocate your manufacturing resources according to customer priorities. This is a fundamental change for most Japanese companies used to thinking of Japan-based *monozukuri* first and how to sell products in foreign markets second.

If, for example, Panasonic had worked backward from the Super Genba structure that I described in my book *Panasonic* into its manufacturing strategy, the first question that would have come to mind would have been, "Where do we locate our plasma and LCD facilities in order to ensure no more than ten days of sales in inventory?" Because it takes only a day and a half to make these products, this should have been easy to do. The result would have optimized Panasonic's ability to turn customer information into cash. Its $20 billion in losses would have been avoided. Sharp, Sony, and others could have made the same simple calculation. If they had done this, today they would be world-beaters instead of the losers they became.

What would leadership have brought? The emerging smarTV market will rival the smart phone market in size and none of these companies will be players in it. Unless they become unbranded, Foxconn-like suppliers to next gen TV winners like Apple, Google, and Amazon.

Note that from the Super Genba point of view, this is not a hard calculation to make. Nothing in the previous paragraphs is remotely complex or obscure. It looks strictly at how big a *genba* we need to accelerate the movement of cash and reason back from there to factory location.

Yet this simple reasoning has proven very difficult for Japanese companies. And the consequences have been devastating. Sharp, for example, should have looked at its high number of days of sales in inventory in the mid-2000s and reasoned that its *genba* was too small. Then it should have asked itself, how big a *genba* do we need to get us to 10 days? And what kind of manufacturing strategy will support this? The answer would not have been a giant LCD factory in Sakai, which, instead of driving days of sales down to a competitive 10 days in inventory, wound up pushing them to a terminal 78 in 2012.

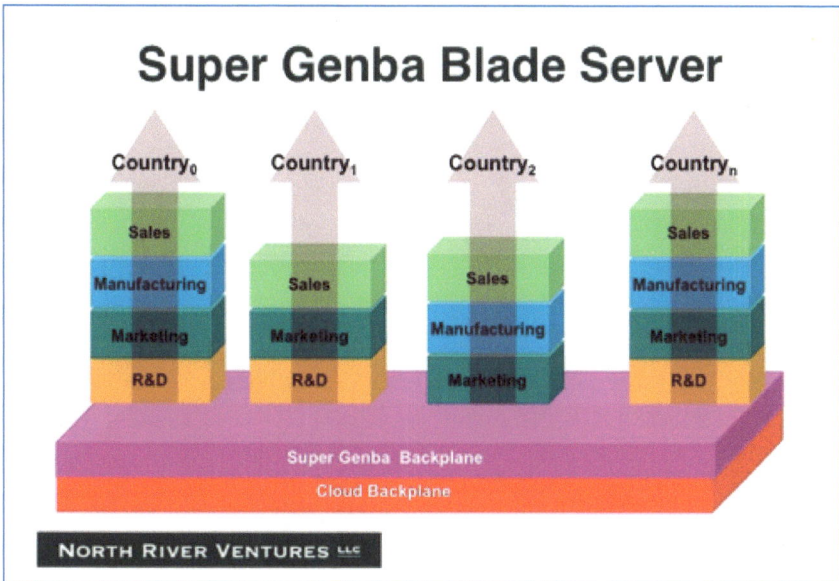

Super Genba Blade Server

Country$_0$ · Sales · Manufacturing · Marketing · R&D

Country$_1$ · Sales · Marketing · R&D

Country$_2$ · Sales · Manufacturing · Marketing

Country$_n$ · Sales · Manufacturing · Marketing · R&D

Super Genba Backplane

Cloud Backplane

NORTH RIVER VENTURES LLC

Why did such a fundamental flaw last so long and why do so many companies have it? This was the question that Sean White and I struggled with twenty-five years ago at NEC. You can see it recurring to this day. Then as now, the only sensible explanation is that by having such huge companies rest on such tiny *genba*, these firms were effectively blinded to changes in the market.

I have asked hundreds of Japanese factory managers over the decades why they persist in large-scale Japan-centric manufacturing and have never gotten a cogent answer.

What should the ideal Super Genba manufacturing strategy look like? The obvious answer is that it should be as close to the customer interface as possible to maximize the rate at which customer information can be turned into cash. For companies whose customers are mostly Japanese, this will be Japan, of course. But, for companies with large overseas markets, it will be as close to those markets as possible.

Collocating manufacturing operations with customers has the effect of expanding the *genba* so that it is big enough to bring in real-time customer information at competitive rates.

What results is something like the chart here: an array of company resources mixed and matched like blades on a server as markets need them.

The server, comprising of the Super Genba and cloud backplanes, holds the firm together. Companies can communicate both horizontally between functions and geographies and vertically, enabling complete support of the *kizuna* inverted pyramid of *Super Genba* Step Two.

You can see here the Super Genba structure enables a shift from the self-contained small United States thinking of the last half century to the multi-vectored large Holland thinking that Japan needs to succeed in this century. This structure goes a long way toward neutralizing the impact of foreign exchange shifts. In banking, this is called "position control," and the sooner manufacturers begin to think of how bankers manage their foreign exchange positions, the sooner they will understand how to structure their manufacturing operations.

Many Japanese factory managers ask, how is distributed manufacturing possible when we need tight control of our operations to ensure competitive yield rates and capacity utilization? The answer is, manufacturing is becoming appified and cloud-based. Therefore, the cloud must be the focus of yield and capacity management. If you've ever been into a giant LCD factory you will see this immediately. These factories are giant clean rooms run on servers with one or two people wandering around in moon suits. There is no reason why the same servers could not run half a dozen smaller facilities around the world closer to markets. This would not only better manage the risks of supply chain disruption for political (China) and seismic (The Great Tohoku Earthquake) reasons, but it would accelerate cash conversion, the primary goal of business.

If, instead of a factory, Sharp had put a server farm at Sakai and Panasonic had done the same at Himeji and Amagasaki, neither firm would have run into the trouble that it did. Not to mention the fixed asset misalignment.

Taken farther, if Panasonic had reasoned from servers back into its 88 business units, a good 80 more than any sentient being can manage, it would have cleaned shop a good half decade before it did. More to the point, it would have understood how to clean shop.

For years I got polite nods, one CEO of a very large company even saying, "McInerney-san has strong ideas!" By this he did not mean good ideas. For many in Japan, huge domestic factories are like industrial temples worthy of the utmost respect. To me, the only question worth asking is, "How much working capital are we wasting to do this?" And then, "How many customers are we losing because we are not close enough to them to know what they need?"

I often see factory managers supporting the requirements of Japan-based product management that has no idea what overseas markets want. In the Introduction I described a week during which team after team came in to present their operations to me. Each one, seemingly without the knowledge of the others, showed sales in Japan going up and going down everywhere else. It occurred to no one to ask why. Still less did anyone ask if other teams had the same problem and maybe ask if there was something systemic going wrong. They all assumed that their overseas sales people were not performing. The idea that their factories were pumping out products for which there was no demand had occurred to no one.

150

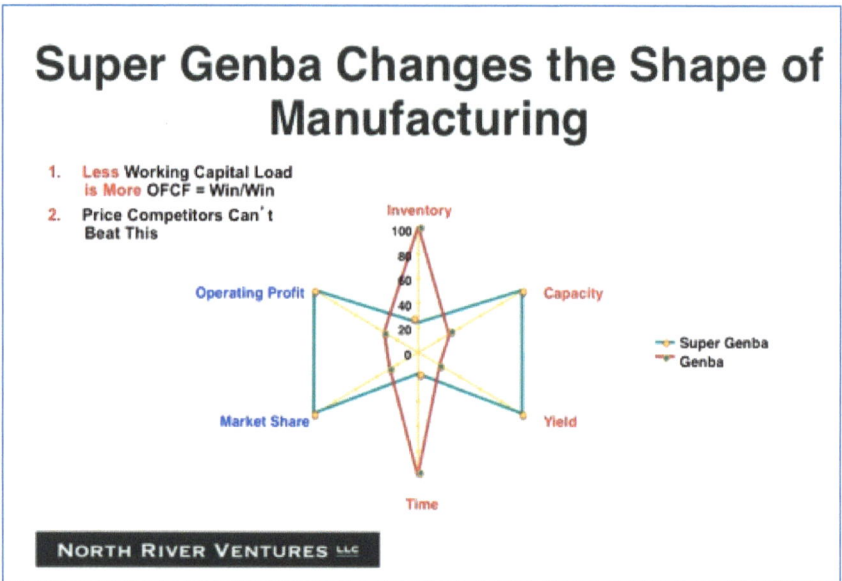

Super Genba Changes the Shape of Manufacturing

1. Less Working Capital Load is More OFCF = Win/Win
2. Price Competitors Can't Beat This

NORTH RIVER VENTURES LLC

Further, in none of these meetings did I meet managers with overseas experience of any depth. In short, no one had the slightest idea of what was going on, either in the markets they were targeting, in how their own operations were managing these, or how other teams were trying to solve the same problem. Knowledge was being shared neither vertically in each silo nor horizontally across silos, something that Lafley and Charan said is fatal. In this case, these teams were from the company's biggest division and it soon racked up the company's biggest losses. A first-class manufacturing operation was destroyed because it was not structured to get and harvest customer information fast enough to turn it into cash at competitive rates.

Here is what your manufacturing operations should look like. You can see that the *genba* and Super Genba structures are markedly different. Even if a *genba* operation were to get high yield and capacity utilization, it would still be deficient in all other key aspects. So concentrating on these two vectors alone would not produce satisfactory results.

The disastrous March 11 earthquake brought this home to many Japanese companies full force as their supply chains collapsed. In some cases whole industries worldwide seized up because of their dependence on ruined Japanese supply chains. In other cases, only Japanese companies were affected and their foreign competitors moved in to take market share. Had my blade server strategy been in place, the affected firms would have continued to sell without a hiccup. Since March 11, it is common to hear CEOs openly discuss the need to distribute supply chains globally.

SUPER GENBA LESSONS

1. You cannot build manufacturing operations on a tiny *genba* and expect to succeed. You will find yourself shipping blindly into your markets and being endlessly surprised at your bad results.

2. Manufacturing is as much a part of Super Genba as is the smallest sales office. It must be thought of that way, designed that way, and operated that way.

SUPER GENBA STEP FIVE: BUILD A SUPERIOR BRAND

Brand is managing your customers' experience of your products. It is therefore core to your ability to turn customer information into cash faster than your competitors. Brand Superiority is doing this so well that you affect outcomes in your market.[45]

Super Genba logic says that as the cloud inflates, supersizing the *genba*, managing customer experience—and therefore brand in the new inflating space—becomes very complex very quickly. As the cloud inflates it becomes ever harder for anyone with a simple *genba* operation to affect outcomes in their markets.

I tell managers that they must build a "brand performance envelope" at cloud scale. I took the expression from the phrase "performance envelope" used to rate military aircraft. This envelope measures aircraft performance on three axes: speed, rate of climb, and turning radius. The fighter with the best numbers gains air superiority and wins.

You can think of the three cloud membranes in *Super Genba* Step One: app, app enablement, and app delivery. Your brand envelope is how well your products and services perform and interact on all three Cloud Membranes. The competitor with top performance in all three gains Brand Superiority and determines outcomes in its markets.

This is why Sony's then-CEO Howard Stringer quickly grasped that *monozukuri* thinking is mistaken. *Monozukuri* is not brandable in the fast-inflating cloud universe because it cannot be measured on any of the axes that describe Brand Superiority in modern markets. But, appified Hyper Monozukuri can be measured this way, which is why Stringer understood that it is so important to achieve.

---

[45] *Brand Superiority*, North River Ventures LLC, October 2000

You can see from the Super Genba viewpoint that brand has little to do with advertising, though ads can support a strong brand. Only once you have built your Super Genba brand performance envelope can you advertise effectively.

Nitto Denko realized that it had a big brand problem. The company had many, many industrial products that, to the untrained eye, had nothing in common. And it was entering markets that appeared to have even less in common. At first blush, this looks like a brand nightmare.

So the Nitto team looked more closely at itself and its customers. One thing was immediately obvious. Another, the most important, was much less so.

What was obvious was that whatever Nitto does is polymer-based. Whether its products are industrial tapes, surface protection films, optoelectronic screens for LCDs and smart phones, medical devices, or anything else it makes, all are polymers in one useful form or another. But, this large range of polymer products, regardless of what they have in common, could prompt Nitto's product groups to express their brand mission in different terms to different customers. Both internal and external cohesion would suffer, effectively unbranding the company. Trying to give the firm a future in the cloud world—appifying its polymers, in effect—would be impossible.

What was not so obvious until the Nitto team did a careful review of all of its operations is that everything Nitto does significantly simplifies its customers businesses. The team could not find a single exception in anything Nitto does.

Written out in full, the Nitto team saw that all its customers in all of its markets worldwide got the same powerful benefits from Nitto:

- Better yield rates
+ Better capacity utilization
+ Fewer days of sales in inventory

- **+** Faster speed to market

- **+** More flexibility than the competition

- **+** Fewer days of sales in receivables

- **+** Better cost control

- **=** Improved P&L and lower working capital load on the balance sheet

It was clear from this that Nitto is in the business of using its polymers to simplify its customers' business processes, producing superior financial results for them. The new mission: We simplify our customers' business processes.

From this new, customer-focused mission, Nitto derived the key operational integration strategies that made it successful. There is no conceptual barrier whatever to appifying any of its polymer products and processes to make the essential partner Nitto even more essential. Its Zensorium Tinké product does exactly this for consumers.

Better still, advertising, marketing, global account operations, R&D, and manufacturing can all focus on one company-wide mission that is easy for customers to understand. We simplify your business. Not only can Nitto train all its people in how its mission works, it can more easily filter good from bad customers. Good customers want the benefits Nitto brings to their income statements and balance sheets through process simplification and will pay Nitto for the value added that they get. These customers are profitable. Bad customers don't see the value of simplified business operations, cannot relate these to their own core financials, and will always be a problem to deal with. They will generate losses and should be derisked.

Without a clear mission that shows clear benefits to customers the way Nitto's does, sales teams could spend years of fruitless effort and even get large market shares, only to lose money doing it.

Today, Nitto can start the conversation with its customers by showing measurable improvements in everything from capacity utilization and yield to working capital management. This is the language of cash velocity that we saw in *Super Genba* Step Two. Discussing Nitto's products and processes with customers in order to identify profitable functions it can perform for them follows them naturally. This is a pole reversal of traditional Japanese hit or miss selling methods, of offering more and more products and hoping that customers choose some.

Nitto's transformation from selling products to selling functions is the essence of the *monozukuri*-to-Hyper Monozukuri transition.

SUPER GENBA LESSONS

1. Brand is managing your customers' experience of your products. Brand is therefore one of the main organizing principles of all successful companies.

2. Gain Brand Superiority by managing your customers' experience of your products so well that you affect outcomes in your markets.

3. Super Genba-style information efficiency makes Super Genba companies the only firms with the physical infrastructure to manage how their customers experience their products twenty-four hours a day, day-in, day-out, anywhere in the world. This turns customers into an annuity stream that can last for decades.

Super Genba Step Six: Manage Human Resources

The Super Genba system sends you information about customers, innovation, cash management, and much more, as we have seen. But, as Sean White and I discovered when we put it in place with our top customers nearly three decades ago, it also tells you whom to employ and where to employ them. The Super Genba system makes it clear who does what, when and where, and so is an excellent driver of Human Resources' priorities.

The Super Genba system pushes so much customer information into management that Human Resources teams can more easily determine what kinds of talent they need and where. They can remap these capabilities onto the company before markets change and the company discovers too late that it has all the wrong people in all the wrong places.

For example, if the Super Genba system tells you that you must operationally integrate with a customer in new ways, you must get the people who can do this in place quickly and integrate them well with your own operation.

Often this means finding the kind of talent the firm does not have and with which it has no experience. Which in turn means hiring new people with a range of experience and seniority.

The Super Genba system assigns managers from all functions from R&D to HQ staff to sales to customers. No one escapes daily interaction with customers. In addition, to manage top customers worldwide, you must use senior executives native to the country where the customer is headquartered. An American for Walmart, a Japanese for Toyota, and a Dutchman for Unilever, for example.

Doing these two things forces you to do several things:

- Identify which human resources go to which customers and where
- Map out which human resource capabilities you are missing
- Identify where and with whom to fill these capability gaps
- Create a compensation plan that rewards your global teams for improving customer performance

These four things seem simple and obvious. But they are not. First, as Unilever discovered, Super Genba accelerates the integration of foreign employees into the upper ranks of management and puts many in line for the top job. Second, Super Genba accelerates the integration of outsiders at all levels of seniority into the company in order to meet fast changing customer needs. Both of these, the integration of foreign employees and outsiders, will be difficult for Japanese firms used to hiring Japanese freshmen out of college, keeping them for their careers, and using on-the-job training techniques that may not be up-to-date or appropriate for fast-moving new markets.

In addition, many such freshmen will not survive the rapid changes in customer needs as the years go by and will have to be let go, another wrenching, but necessary, change for Japanese companies.

Another big problem is commitments to lifetime employment that Japanese employees get but that foreigners in the same company do not. This splits firms into two camps with unlike motivations that work in perverse and always value-destructive ways.

For example, the overseas employees facing the constant threat of dismissal yet without the chance to run the company which makes taking such risks worthwhile often become collections of underperformers. Their philosophy: Keep your head down and hope to last long enough to reach retirement. I tell CEOs of these companies that they are running retirement funds, not companies. They don't like to hear this, but it is true and they need to face up to what this means for sales and profit performance.

I have also seen the opposite. Vigorous overseas employees coupled with a domestic Japanese operation that knows that it cannot be dismissed and has no motivation whatever. The result is the same, of course. This asymmetry can be run either way but it will generate dismal sales and profits.

The key is a symmetric operation where everyone is measured and rewarded the same way.

The biggest change by far will be integrating women. The lack of women in management is Japan's biggest weakness today. Men and women think differently, providing many solutions to problems that either would not think of alone. Combine these and we get more and better solution sets faster than with men or women by themselves. If you go into world markets using only half the brainpower available to you and only that of men, your risk of product failure goes through the roof.

In addition, many customers worldwide are women—half the consuming market for starters—and more and more of the world's biggest and most innovative companies, like IBM, are run by women and have many women in all levels of management. You cannot send all-male teams to sell to these customers. Well, you can. And you will get the result that you planned for.

One of my favorite things to do in Japan is to ask in a meeting full of TV product managers if anyone knows a woman stupid enough to design a TV remote control. Then I pull out my iPhone with its smooth cloud management interface and say, "women, lots of women."

This says it all.

My question to every Japanese manager is, "Why increase your risks of failure to such high levels when you don't have to?" I have never had a clear answer, though I've had some foolish ones. A manager of a team that had not had a world-beater in a couple of decades once snorted that he didn't need a woman to tell him to make his product in pink. I told him that, on the contrary, he needed women to make sure that his product worked well enough to win in the market. He could never have worked for me because he would not have made it past his first job interview.

I always had a lot of women in my operation, one reason why we dominated our markets worldwide. Which, in turn, is why McGraw-Hill walked in to my New York office one day at twenty minutes notice and bought my company from me. I was thirty-eight.

A few years ago, I was sitting in the Azalea restaurant in the Osaka New Otani having breakfast and reading a paper. A young waitress came up to me and, in a faultless American accent and American-to-American intonation and facial expressions, asked me if I would like some coffee. I have spent as much as three months a year at the New Otani and know that, while the lobby staff all speak excellent English, the restaurant staff speak only a few words, at most. I was shocked.

I asked her where she had learned to speak English so well. Megumi Minami was then a student at Kwansei Gakuin University and told me that she had learned English in high school but was mostly self-taught. I kept up with Meg as she went through college, studied for a year abroad at Nebraska Wesleyan University, graduated, returned home and began looking for a job in Japan. What is astonishing to me about Meg is that you would think you are talking to an American, not to a Japanese who speaks English. This, I realized, was an exceptionally valuable talent that no company wants to pass up. I circulated her name and résumé.

Yet it proved very difficult for me—and I am not exactly unknown in Japan—to get her interviews, and what interviews I could get for her were done in Japanese, likely by people in no position to evaluate what her multilingual, multicultural talent might do for their companies. She got no offers. Finally, she got herself an interview with a company that had the smarts to interview her in English. They were as amazed as I was by her prodigious linguistic talent and offered her a job by cell phone on her way home from the interview. They will soon find that her French isn't bad either. Some of the biggest companies in Japan missed one of the biggest talents they will ever come across. This is not how you run a successful business.

Because the Super Genba system is customer-driven, not vendor-driven, and because all over the world there are women CEOs, executives, and managers, selling to them means that the Super Genba teams must be diverse. It is because of the power of the Super Genba customer interface that women will be accelerated through Japanese management. A Super Genba structure without women isn't super and will fail.

How fast can Japan make this switch to teams integrated well enough to keep up with global customers? Very fast. Roughly seventy-four percent of Japanese women with a university education leave their jobs voluntarily, compared to thirty-one percent in the U.S. and thirty-five percent in Germany. Few do this because they want to start a family; most because they feel that their careers have been stymied.[46] This is a huge reserve army that Japanese companies could put to work in just a few months.

Some seventy-seven percent of these women want to return to work, but only forty-three percent succeed compared to seventy-three percent in the U.S. and sixty-eight percent in

---

[46] Hewlett, Sylvia Ann, and Laura Sherbin. "Off-Ramps and On-Rams Japan: Keeping Talented Women on the Road to Success." Center for Work-Life Policy, October 2011

Germany. Worse, forty-four percent of these end up in dead-end career, earning less than before they left.

This poor performance is, in my view, a major explanation of Japan's near quarter century economic stall. The lack of women has thrown product and service development into a tailspin from which it is getting harder and harder for Japan to recover.

Kathy Matsui at Goldman Sachs reported that if Japan could mobilize its reserve army of educated women, its labor force would grow by 8.2 million and its gross domestic product increase by fifteen percent.[47] With so much upside, why would anyone not want to do this? Shinzo Abe agrees.[48]

In addition, there are the high costs of replacing highly educated and trained women who leave the workplace. Only to repeat the same costly, time-consuming process over and over every few years when they leave.

These data are so marked that the consulting firm McKinsey and Company has decided that one of the smartest things a company can do is recruit from the reserve army of women who have left the firm and bring their talents back into the fold.[49] These women are smart, know the operation and its customers, and can add value quickly in all the right places.

The same can be said of including non-Japanese in all levels of decision-making: it's all about minimizing risk by maximizing the inflow of high value customer information and matching this to top talent.

[47] Matsui, Kathy. "Womenomics 3.0: The Time Is Now." Goldman Sachs, October 1, 2010

[48] Abe, Shinzo. "Shinzo Abe: Unleashing the Power of 'Womenomics'." *The Wall Street Journal* 25 Sept. 2013

[49] Kwoh, Leslie. "McKinsey Tries to Recruit Mothers Who Left the Fold." *The Wall Street Journal*, February 19, 2013

As my longtime colleague and HR expert Danny Kalman says, capability mapping on a global scale is vital to the execution of corporate strategy. Do it wrong and failure is preordained. Nitto Denko CEO Yukio Nagira sees it the same way: Without this capability mapping, he says, "We can't compete in the next stage of globalization."

There are many people who say that this can never be done in Japan. Not so. Recently, I have seen huge strides by Nitto Denko to create unified global management. These efforts are paying off in record operating profits and a broad base of refreshing innovation from labs around the world full of women and Japanese and non-Japanese employees all pushing as hard as they can. There is no doubt in my mind that this commitment to a unified, global corporate culture will be a winner. Most of Nitto's innovations, and there are many, can easily double the size of the whole company. Nitto reduces the risk of not finding a sales doubling success because of the way in which the company manages its human resources.

SUPER GENBA LESSONS

- Map your human resources from your customers back into the company, not from the company out to the customers.
- Make sure that you have enough women in management to work eye-to-eye with your top customers worldwide.

SUPER GENBA STEP SEVEN: DESIGN YOUR ORGANIZATION

Let us now see what a Super Genba organization looks like. Customers, as the chart shows, drive the entire structure. On the right you have customers ranked in a sales pyramid with the broadest number, usually small, and often consumers, on the bottom. At the top is the small number of very large global customers.

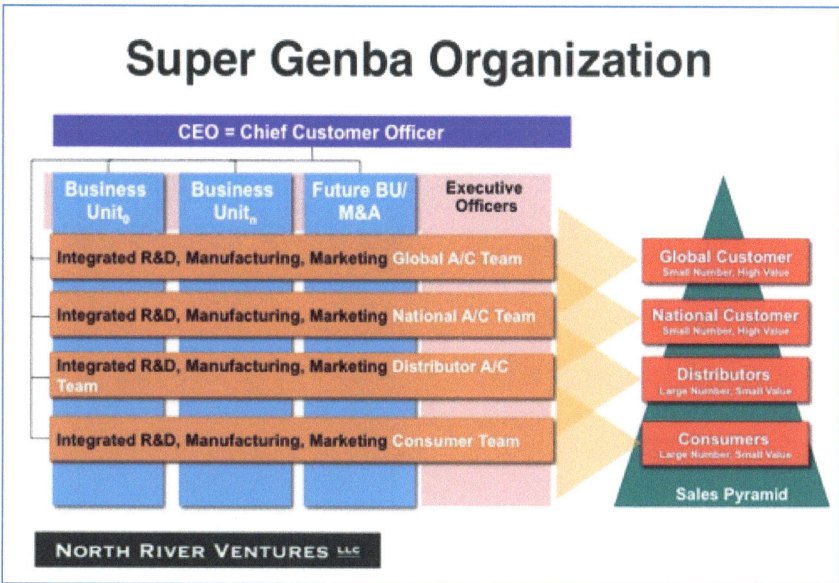

Running across all business units to the customer are the fully integrated *kizuna* sales operations I described in *Super Genba* Step Two. All of these, like the business units, report to the CEO. The CEO gets customer information flowing from all directions and cannot miss much whether from a BU or a sales team. The CEO is the Chief Customer Officer

From the left you see arrayed business units from 0 to n and a slot for future M&A. You can grow organically, merge, or demerge. You can have one business unit or a half dozen. You can operate in one country or many. The structure still holds.

of the company. Everyone in every BU is in the Super Genba customer interface.

For each large global customer, there is a Global Account Management team run by a senior executive from the country where the account is headquartered. A GAM team selling to Toyota would be headed by a Japanese and run from Nagoya. A GAM team selling to Walmart would be headed by an American and based in Bentonville, Arkansas. And so on for the firm's top customers. Management should also target new, strategic customers with embryonic teams ready to exploit opportunities with a full GAM once there is a sales opening.

The CEO, as the Chief Customer Officer, should be able to monitor all these top accounts daily with something like Salesforce.com. CEOs of GAM customers should have the Chief Customer Officer's direct phone and e-mail for immediate problem resolution.

Next in the structure are National Accounts. These are single country customers, not multinationals, that can be supported by a team run in the country in which the customer is based. Below these are distributors who should always be reserved for small customers, especially small businesses. Distributors may also be of value in retail settings as Apple has demonstrated.

Finally, there is the large, fast-moving, cloud-born consumer sector to which direct sales are vital. This sector requires a specialized team that understands how to sell to consumers. There are two companies to follow here. Apple, of course, with its hugely successful Apple Stores. And Proctor and Gamble because, even though it sells only through retailers, it does an enormous amount of ethnography. CEO A.G. Lafley likes to talk about how, whenever he travels around the world, he spends time in the home of a consumer to see how P&G customers use P&G products. This, he says, ensures that all the ethnology teams at P&G stay focused on what customers really want. "We're not curing cancer," he told a gathering of my fellow University of Toronto alumni in New York in March 2013. "We get maybe fifteen seconds of your time every day and we want to make those seconds easier."

The elegance of the customer-focused Super Genba structure is that it works for any number of business units with any type of customer from consumer to global industrial empire. One structure embraces all your business units and all of your customers, wherever they are. It scales up and down and left to right, from small to large, from local to global.

If supported by strong cloud-based IT, Super Genba allows your company to inflate like a balloon, maintaining its surface geometry as it grows. This is vital to being able to double sales profitably at cloud scale.

And, it's field-proven. When I first started working with this structure for a company in the U.S. in 1990, we landed $2.5 billion in sales in eighteen months: $500 million to one customer and $1 billion each to two others. Better still, in each case these sales were twice what the company expected to get before we restructured Super Genba style.

When I've worked on these systems in Japan, however, the first problem we have is that the GAM teams find that they have very low-level contacts. This means two things. The company doesn't know its customers, whether industrial, commercial, or consumer, well enough to understand their deepest needs. Second, companies and their customers do not have adequate C-Level relationships, CEO-to-CEO, CFO-to-CFO etc.

As customer needs change, mispositioned companies are often the last to find out about these changes and frequently find themselves losing large amounts of business. An excellent example is how the shift from hard disks in computers and lap tops to solid state memory caught hard disk suppliers unaware, leaving them with no one to whom to sell and nothing to sell, a double hit.

The Super Genba structure is designed to prevent that. You should know so much about your customers that you are the best informed among your competitors. This is simple math. The size of the customer interface is designed so that customer information hits all ranks and functions of your operations equally, giving you the best chance to get as many of your best people as possible working on customer solutions faster than the competition.

The solution, using the Super Genba structure, is to identify high-level weaknesses and fix them fast. The CEO should take charge of this, making sure that customer contacts are maintained at the right level 24/7.

You will find that Super Genba quickly exposes enormous differences in customers in the same market. As described in *Super Genba* Step Two, in only a few minutes into Nitto Denko's first GAM meetings, it saw large differences in customer sophistication that were not previously apparent to management. Nitto learned enough early enough to move quickly to increase sales efforts to its more profitable and less-risky customers.

The Super Genba structure says that to develop new business, you must identify a small number of large target customers and focus an embryonic *kizuna* team on each. Doing this is low cost and effective business development. All the best people get to see the best strategic customers personally and work together to decide what they can do to add value to these customers. The most and least profitable customers will quickly separate themselves, and management can make decisions with the best upside potential.

One of the biggest challenges in Super Genba, as your human resources people will tell you as soon as they look at my chart, is compensation. In Super Genba, the BUs hold the P&L so, in some ways, very little changes. But the *kizuna* teams must be compensated across BUs and across geographies for their successes. It is not unusual to find, however, that Japanese companies can have as many BU-based comp plans in the same country as they have BUs operating there. Resolving these is not easy and takes professional advice from compensation specialists.

Also, you may have to change your invoicing system. It is common for *monozukuri* companies to have no way of invoicing for an ongoing Hyper Monozukuri relationship. I was at one meeting where an American engineer said, "We want to own the project for 20 years." His Japanese colleagues did not understand what he meant. They could invoice only for products, not a relationship. His solution in this case was to form a separate, minority-owned, subsidiary with outside partners that could be reported outside the business units on the P&L as Other Income. That is unnecessarily complex.

Another big challenge is talent or capability mapping as we saw in *Super Genba* Step Six. You will find that, as you get closer to customers and their needs, you have weaknesses in your talent. You will also find that there are large gaps where you have no one who does what is needed. These gaps must be filled quickly and integrated with the rest of the company. Doing this requires special expertise.

A major benefit is in succession planning. Daily pressure from customers forces the best managers to the surface, making it easier to identify the next generation of top managers in the company.

SUPER GENBA LESSONS

1. Businesses designed to bring more of their operations to bear on their customers gain more market share more profitably than others.

SUPER GENBA STEP EIGHT: MANAGE IT

Because Super Genba is all about accelerating your ability to turn customer information into cash faster than your competition, it shows you where to spend on Information Technology and why. The challenge is to do this while the *genba* is expanding at cloud scale.

To turn customer information into cash fast enough to be competitive today, you need several cloud-based tools:

- Big Data on customers
- Real time supply chain management
- Real time customer relations management

First and foremost, IT is about transmitting customer information through the supply chain and back to customers to minimize cash wait states in inventory and receivables. In other words, IT is the cash engine of the company.

Ask yourself a simple question: How much is a day of sales in our company? For Sony a day is $176 million and a month, $5.3 billion. How much would you spend on IT to free up this kind of cash? What would your choices look like if you had this cash?

A smart manager would put in place the IT to free up the balance sheet, and with the resulting information, figure out where to put factories and other operations. Such a manager would set aggressive goals for days of sales in inventory and receivables, then design the company IT to meet those goals.

Having an IT system that shortens days of sales in receivables and inventories maximizes a company's customer-to-supplier information, shortening decision cycles, derisking products, and lightening the balance sheet. Sharp, as we saw, did the opposite, investing heavily to launch products into a customer-to-supply chain information void. This put the entire company at risk.

It is common in Japan to view IT as a cost that must be minimized. As a result, many Japanese companies do not use cloud services to generate the Big Data on customers that they need to launch products successfully and keep customers once they are won. They cannot manage their customer relationships, have not invested in the bandwidth to manage telepresence conferences internally or with their customers, and often do not have uniform global billing and product database systems. IT is an afterthought that these firms drag along with them, spending a few yen only when they absolutely have to and sometimes not even then. Japanese IT systems are often Balkanized between countries and often company operating divisions within countries run heterodox, incompatible systems with conflicting goals.

When in Japan on a visit a few years ago, I received a wonderful electric shaver as a gift from Panasonic. It was the very latest model and had all the features I could ever want. Sounds good, right? Some time later I needed to replace a part and e-mailed Panasonic's good customer relations folks in the U.S. with the product number and asked for the part, credit card at the ready. They were as polite as possible but had no record of such a product and asked me where I got it. Rather than embarrass them beyond measure by saying who, exactly, had given it to me, I simply said that I had bought the shaver in Japan. Well, they said, they only had U.S. product and part numbers; there was no universal product database. Identical products have different model and parts numbers according to market. In their world, my product did not exist so there was nothing that they could do.

For the lack of something as simple as a global product database, Panasonic had effectively unbranded itself.

Any human on the planet could have bought any one of Panasonic's almost unthinkable range of products—it has admitted to 88 business units and "perhaps even a million" products[50]—moved to any other part of the planet and had the same problem that I had. Scale my simple part number question to a million products from 88 business units and do it without a unified database. The sheer size of the IT problem becomes immediately evident. Panasonic's subsequent $20 billion loss is not surprising.

What is surprising is that Panasonic survived for as long as it did having so many products in so many markets. Especially since, when it admitted to perhaps a million products, it also said that it had never actually counted them. Let's do the math. Take Panasonic's sales, divide them by a million, and you get an average of 146 iPads worth in sales per product per year. Suppose Panasonic's number is out by an order of magnitude in the company's favor. This gives 14,600 iPads worth of sales per product per year. But, Apple sells something like 85,000,000 iPads a year. How can anyone scale a company profitably with per product sales so tiny? All for the lack of an IT system that tells management where it is in real time.

This is clearly a case of *monozukuri* gone very, very wrong, an endless array of uneconomic products being pumped straight into a demand vacuum. And yet, managers in Japan are often proud of the vast range of choices they offer their customers. Many will say, in English, that product proliferation offers "total solutions" to their customers. But this is a misreading of what the word "solution" means in English. A solution solves a customer operational problem the way Nitto Denko does. It is a processes that integrates a supplier into a key part of customer operations, adding value directly. It does not mean offering an endless array of bits and pieces that are supposed to add up to something called a solution. Quite the reverse: Doing this is adding to the problem.

---

[50] Tabuchi, Hiroko. "As Some Vow to Scale Back, Panasonic Pushes Vast Catalog." *The New York Times*, July 12, 2010, sec. Business / Global Business

The core risk to Japanese companies is in having very large but fractured fronts facing the outside world without the tools needed to harvest the opportunities of the Zetabyte Era. Nothing could be more risky.

An analyst looking at Panasonic's annual report working capital data, for example, could infer, whether or not this is the case, that it does not have an IT system that connects the supply chains for its many products and business units to customers. If you were an investor, you would be out of the stock.

Put another way, a low Management Grade tells investors that a company does not have competitive IT.

Since human beings are rational and do not want to drive into the grave the companies that provide their livelihoods, there can be only one possible answer. Companies in such trouble are in an information vacuum. They do not have enough information to know that they are in mortal danger. To all intents and purposes, they have no IT. Or, put another way, what IT they do have is of no value. When we add the demands of the Zetabyte Era to the picture, this is terminal.

An example of how dangerous this can be is the common obsession of Japanese consumer electronics companies with the South Korean company Samsung. When I look at Samsung, however, I see impending disaster. *Super Genba* says that imitating Samsung is a big mistake.

Why? Samsung has a combined 80 days of sales in inventory and receivables against Apple's 30. That's nearly two months in hard cash. Samsung is four days of sales worse off than Apple was in 1997, a year before Tim Cook kicked off the cash velocity revolution there. This tells me that Samsung's supply chain and sales operations are not competitive. Indeed, Samsung's data show that its sales operations began to fall apart in 2001 and have not recovered, making it a weak, not a strong competitor. *Super*

Genba shows that it could take Samsung 10 to 15 years to catch up. *Super Genba* also says that no one has ever managed to do this even with the full 15 years in which to do it.

The data say that Samsung's sales, R&D, and manufacturing operations are not integrated at the sales front end of the company and that global account management in any useful form does not exist. Samsung has no direct sales presence, no cloud-born Big Data on customers, and so no ability to manage its brand.

Where, for example, are Samsung's server farms to compete with Apple's North Carolina iCloud operation? What if Apple uses its cash and server farms to transform itself into a Netflix on steroids? Think Disney as an app. Then Samsung will be an iCloud slave. And all the app revenues will go to Apple's App Store. Samsung has yet to enter any of the Hyper Monozukuri markets that will determine its future.

Looking farther down the line, Samsung faces the same growth problem that Apple does: How many markets are big enough to double its sales? Health care and automotive are the top two. As I said in Part One, Apple is sure to be well advanced on an iCar, and Google has something similar. Big and location data dominate the thinking of both companies. They see cars as cloud access devices on wheels, and could upend the brand order in automotive in a short time. Samsung competing with world number four Hyundai in tight knit South Korea? Not likely.

This leaves medical. Medical too is cloud- and Big Data-driven, exactly what Samsung is not.

What are Samsung's options? It has $40 billion in cash, about a quarter of Apple's stash. This is not enough to buy Google with its price tag of over $290 billion, which is what it would take to profit from Android working across Samsung's existing and future platforms. Everywhere you look in Big Data, the dominators have paths to the future along which Samsung offers little.

So, why focus on Samsung? Because the Japanese CE sector does not have the customer data or the IT to understand customers and puts its attention instead on a flailing competitor. Following a competitor that is on the same dead-end track and a good decade and a half behind the market is not a good use of management time. There is not a scintilla of evidence that Samsung knows how big the hole is that it has dug for itself nor even that it knows that it is in a hole. This alone should tell Japanese CE managers to give their attention to their customers. Without sufficient IT, though, this is the one thing that they cannot do.

There are solutions to problems as big as these. Simple cloud-based overlays like Salesforce.com that require no change in existing systems can be put into place quickly. These force to the surface one of the biggest unknowns in the information vacuum: Who are our biggest customers? A CEO can see and act on this information within a quarter of installing Salesforce at the most, and quickly begin to sort out some of the basics of where the company adds value and for whom. Top managers can drill down to small details on critical accounts if need be. This way, management can stay ahead of customer problems, maximize revenues, and identify new opportunities before the competition can. Without spending a lot.

About thirty years ago, Sean White and I faced a big sales problem at our first company, the publisher Northern Business Information. We knew a lot about how many products we were selling but little about to whom. To figure this out we had to compile the data by hand, a long and tedious process.

Our solution was to outsource all our sales and accounting data to a prototypical cloud service, ADP. We saw immediately what we did not know: who our top customers were and what they were buying from us. We could also see

174

who was not buying from us, large lost opportunities. From this data we were able to work with our sales and project management teams in tandem to boost sales to our most profitable accounts. We also built strong business with customers we had missed simply because we didn't know that we had missed them. With a little bit of outsourced IT we turned our information vacuum into a profit engine that McGraw-Hill soon bought from us.

I often tell Japanese managers trying to hold together global operations through endless business trips that their goal should be to put JAL and ANA out of business. Do your jet lag at home, I tell them, and get your IT systems to do the traveling for you. Why spend twelve to fourteen hours in a plane between Tokyo and New York, longer if your operation is somewhere in Japan from which there are no direct flights, when you can push a button and have whole global teams on high definition telepresence panels right in your office? All without spending money and time on redesigning malfunctioning IT platforms.

Do this right and your IT priorities will be obvious. This will allow you to avoid costly and time-consuming IT re-engineering done in the dark.

Yet my friends at Cisco and Salesforce.com tell me that their biggest business in Japan is with foreign companies located there and that selling to Japanese companies is harder than they expected given the cost benefits of what they offer.

Another easy-to-use cloud service is LinkedIn, the best sales tool I know of. You should never target a customer without making sure that the whole team knows who knows whom. LinkedIn is the simplest, fastest, and cheapest way to do this.[51]

---

[51] Hempel, Jessi. "LinkedIn: How It's Changing Business (and How to Make It Work for You)." *Fortune*, June 13, 3013

Perhaps the most damaging space in the information vacuum of Japanese companies is their lack of Big Data. Imagine that you are a Google, Amazon, Apple, or other top global performer today. You are standing on a fast-growing globe of Big Data and looking out at a set of hardware satellites like TVs, smart phones and cars. You understand in a second that Big Data is the gravitational force that holds those satellites in orbit, not the other way around. But all the once-great Japanese consumer electronics brands, standing on their satellites, assume, pre-Copernicus, that everything else orbits them.

Whatever the reasons that so many top Japanese brands ran into trouble—and there are a few as we have seen—their lack of Big Data means they are blind in critical cloud dimensions that determine their futures. Sony had great success in pre-cloud products like the Walkman, and in the transition PlayStation with its dedicated network, but none in today's cloud-driven Big Data-dependent app universe of integrated smartphones, PCs, tablets and smarTVs. Predictably, Sony's once great consumer electronics brand has more or less vanished at the rate at which the cloud inflated.

What makes the Sony story all the more poignant is that, as Sean White and I wrote twenty years ago in *Beating Japan*, Sony co-founder Akio Morita got all the basics right decades before Apple, Google, or anyone else. He foresaw that hardware, content, and communications would blend into an entirely new space where they would leverage each other in a Cloud Membrane-like codependence. This is why Steve Jobs always revered Morita. But illness took him from Sony twenty years before Apple invoked the iCloud to make his vision a reality. After Morita, Sony did not follow his logic to evolve its business model for the Zetabyte Era and the rest, as they say, is history.

In one of the saddest misinterpretations of Morita that I ever read, Kunimasa Suzuki, head of Sony Mobile told France's

Le Figaro that because Sony's Xperia smart phones connect to Sony's QX lens cameras from another Sony division, the company had broken down its internal silos. "What matters," he said "is that this is a Sony product."[52] This is nonsense. The Xperia runs Android. It is a Google product with a Sony label on it.

In the late 1990s Sean White and I created the Palo Alto-based venture incubator CenComV with partner Bell Canada, among others. I remember taking a team of top Bell executives to meet Sony's PlayStation team in Silicon Valley. The idea was to propose embedding the PlayStation in Bell's network offerings. If this worked, we planned to walk the system into other carriers worldwide. It would have been the beginning, had the path been followed, of a way to Sony-wide, cloud-based Big Data systems. We were greeted with incomprehension. Today, Sony's customers are the ones reacting with incomprehension. You know the rest.

SUPER GENBA LESSONS

- Do not operate in an information vacuum. Companies interact with customers on the cloud. Cloud-born Big Data are the eyes with which to see customers. So, no cloud-based Big Data, no interaction. No interaction, no sales.

---

[52] Bembaron, Elsa. "Sony Vise La Place de Numéro Trois Des Smartphones," *Le Figaro*, September 5, 2013

SUPER GENBA STEP NINE: MANAGE MERGERS AND ACQUISITIONS

Many companies use acquisition as the centerpiece of their growth strategy. But, because the purpose of business is to turn customer information into cash faster than competition, mergers can only be accretive between companies with high Cash and Capital Velocity Indices. So, the first thing you have to do when thinking about growing through M&A is to restructure your operations thoroughly enough to get my Management A Grade. Combining low-grade companies is always value destructive. There are no exceptions.

I will give you three examples here of what not to do, one American, one European, and one Japanese. They are so painful that I hope they dissuade you from ever making an acquisition without Super Genba reform first.

The problem is simple enough to describe. We already saw what happened when Compaq bought DEC in 1998. Then, in 2002, Hewlett-Packard bought Compaq, the number one PC supplier in the world, to sustain growth in its PC and server businesses.[53] It also put large sums of R&D into capturing a business outside computing—printers—yet its stock went nowhere. At around the same time, Apple, by contrast, added two innovations—iTunes and iPod—to get out of a declining market for personal computers in which it had a small share, and its stock went through the roof.

In the decade following the Compaq deal, Hewlett went through four CEOs, losing three in ugly dismissals. It acquired EDS for its services and 3Com for its routers, mulled getting out of the PC business, and did a troubled deal for software company Autonomy. While sales are up over two times since buying Compaq, Hewlett's stock which then traded at about $16.50, was in the same place as 2013 began. The Dow was up 40% over the same period. With

---

[53] http://en.wikipedia.org/wiki/Market_share_of_leading_PC_vendors

the Compaq deal, Hewlett's engine of value creation imploded and the company appears rudderless.

What happened? Neither Hewlett nor Compaq lacked resources or imagination. Both companies had huge market share successes. But their shareholders did not benefit.

I use Super Genba to evaluate mergers all the time. The process is simple. This is what H-P should have done:

1. Restructured to gain scalable Super Genba Cash and Capital Velocity Indices and my Management Grade A

2. Examined ten years of the same data on Compaq

3. From these, identified strengths and weaknesses in Compaq's supply chain and sales operations

4. Mapped its own Super Genba operations onto Compaq's to gauge the risks of post-merger integration

This way, Hewlett would have had a very good idea of where the downside and upside were and whether or not it could have made a merger with Compaq accretive. This should have taken no more than a day to do and could have been completed by just two people working for the Chief Strategy Officer.

Hewlett-Packard did none of this. The Compaq deal was announced in early September 2001. On September 17th, 2001 I published my Cash Velocity Index analysis that showed the deal was doomed.

Here is what I wrote:

"H-P takes a staggering 91 days more than Dell to turn a sale into cash. Even if Carly Fiorina applied Dell's methods as fast as Michael Dell did, Hewlett-Packard would find itself in September 2006 roughly where Dell was in June 1996, more than ten years previously. Needless to say, H-P's outlook is grim.

On paper, the combined H-P/Compaq will lop 13 days off H-P's cash conversion cycle. But history's lessons can be harsh. When Compaq acquired DEC, Compaq was 36 days behind Dell and DEC was 64 days behind. The combination quickly came to look like DEC, rather than Compaq—hence Compaq's current woes."[54]

Hewlett's Cash Velocity Index had improved somewhat in the 1996-2001 period. But, without Compaq, H-P would have had to devote all its energies to catching up to Dell, then the Cash Velocity Index leader in the sector. This further assumes that H-P could do as well as Dell did from 1996 on when Dell decided to increase its Cash Velocity Index by applying its system of integrated distribution. My Cash Velocity Index showed that, going flat out, by 2007 H-P would lag behind where Dell was in 2001 by 15 points.

The question the data pose is whether or not a company with H-P's low Cash Velocity Index could catch up fast enough to beat the sector leader before being overwhelmed. This is the question all Apple's competitors in Japan's consumer electronics sector face today. My Cash Velocity Index suggests not.

What did this tell us about H-P's realistic alternatives?

- First, without Super Genba operations, acquisitions were out of the question.

- Second, *genba* business as usual would not work much better.

The Index also shows that improvement means nothing unless you are in the top grade end of the scale.

H-P moved far on the scale, but never reached top grade, so M&A could not possibly be accretive. The Compaq deal,

---

[54] *Hewlett Packard and Compaq* North River Ventures LLC, September 17, 2001

and all the others that followed, did nothing for H-P shareholders.

Moreover, the acquisition of Compaq by H-P significantly worsened H-P's competitive position because Compaq's Cash Velocity Index went increasingly negative during the years before its acquisition by H-P. Thus, it was obvious to me in 2001 that H-P's position would decline once the deal was done, guaranteeing that buying Compaq would end in failure, which it did.

When Compaq acquired DEC several years earlier, Compaq's position was weak though improving, while DEC's was deteriorating rapidly. The combined firm took on the characteristics, not of Compaq, but of DEC. The result was a quick fall off in value and Compaq's putting itself on the block.

This was easy to predict at the time, as I did.[55] What was really interesting, therefore, was H-P's willingness to make the same mistake several years later. The Super Genba System is so unforgiving in this regard that it takes a very naïve CEO indeed to second-guess it. Carly Fiorina was astonishingly naïve and lost her job as a result.

The widely advertised justification for the Hewlett-Packard/Compaq deal was that their combined positions in a range of markets from PCs to servers would make the merged company number one in all of them. This is the same logic used by many companies and it is wrong.

It is not combined market share that makes or breaks value. It is the relative Cash Velocity Indices of the merged parties.

By breaking this Super Genba rule, most mergers destroy shareholder value. These acquisitions, because they do nothing to accelerate the rate at which customer information

---

[55] *Breaking the Moore Time Barrier*, North River Ventures LLC, February 1998

is turned into cash, make Brand Superiority impossible to achieve.

I question why investment bankers counseled so many gigantic mergers in recent decades. I suspect that the lure of banking fees overwhelmed good judgment.

My 2001 analysis showed that Compaq was likely to go under in less than two years, saving H-P the trouble of buying it. So there was no point in thinking that a combination with Compaq would create a sustainable market share advantage. Predictably, only six months after acquiring Compaq in order to have a PC market share greater than market leader Dell's, Hewlett-Packard lost its top spot to Dell. It took Hewlett nearly half a decade to regain its position and half a decade later it was talking about divesting the PC business.[56]

What you see in this example is that the effects of poorly matched Cash Velocity Indices can roil merged companies for many years. This saga has been going on for a decade and a half. And it is far from the only deal to suffer from such long-term effects.

In May 2001, before Alcatel and Lucent merged, I published my view that there would be problems with the deal because of mismatched Cash Velocity Indices. Alcatel had sales of €26 billion but a dizzying 117 days of sales in receivables (competitor Cisco had 31), meaning that its operation was in chaos from one end to the other.[57] By 2012, sales of the combined firms had fallen 46%, to €14 billion. Cumulative operating losses were €20 billion, or 1.4 times 2012 revenues. Two CEOs lost their jobs for failing to fix this.

---

[56] Worthen, Ben, Justin Scheck, and Gina Chon. "H-P Explores Quitting Computers as Profits Slide." *Wall Street Journal*, August 19, 2011, sec. Business Technology

[57] *Alcatel & Lucent*, North River Ventures LLC, May 21, 2001

I could add many other failed deals, like Daimler and Chrysler and Sears and Kmart, where mismatched Cash Velocity Indices allowed me to predict—in a minute or two—implosion well before events. The failure of Circuit City was another easy call.

Here is an example from Japan. As I wrote in the Introduction, in 2008 I said that Sanyo would be a disastrous acquisition for anyone. The data showed that its supply chain and sales operations—everything, basically—were a mess. These numbers had not materially improved for years, indicating that management was neither paying attention nor had the talent to fix its problems.

Taking on Sanyo would require a huge investment in new systems and management time. Meanwhile its sales were declining—28% during the previous five years—and its ability to generate profit was evaporating. If this company were to be brought back to health, the job would have to be done in no more than a year. Few of its existing managers would survive this process. But how would they be replaced? The number of people with the expertise to solve problems as deep as these is tiny.

Panasonic bought Sanyo anyway and discovered that the Cash Velocity Index is destiny.

Panasonic's data were better than Sanyo's, but not by much. This indicated that, even though Panasonic was many times the size of Sanyo, it did not have the systems or management talent to undertake a Super Genba transformation of Sanyo. Marrying the two could not possibly work. This merger would destroy value and probably a lot of it. And did.

The lesson of Hewlett-Packard, Alcatel-Lucent, Daimler-Chrysler, and Sears and Kmart is that the impact of flawed mergers last a decade, maybe more. But, a decade from now, the market will have moved far, far ahead.

There is a deeper lesson. If, as I said, you follow the trail from DEC to Compaq to Hewlett-Packard, it is unlikely that any of the due diligence or investment banking teams advising on these transactions ever looked at comparing cash velocity data. In the Sanyo case, by contrast, Panasonic had access to my model since the day I developed it in 2001. I published the model in *Panasonic* in 2007. Panasonic ignored the guidelines Kirk Nakamura and I had carefully prepared for it and paid a huge price.

This brings me to a key observation about low Cash Velocity Index deals. Because the *genba* of one party does not expand the *genba* of the other, they compound their problems by the square of the number of customers acquired. If this sounds like an exaggeration, think about for a little bit. You will find yourself nodding in agreement.

So, if you want accretive mergers, make sure that you are a Super Genba company first. Focus your due diligence team on the Cash Velocity Indices of the company you want to acquire. Carefully map everything that you do to achieve Super Genba onto what you know of your target's operations. Ask:

- Can we leverage our operations with the target's fast enough to scale profitably?
- Are some of its weaknesses too great to overcome?
- Will the target go under if we don't do a deal, saving us the effort?
- Does the target have Cash Velocity Index skills and capabilities that we don't and that, mapped onto ours, would move us ahead fast?

Underperforming targets can kill the value of a deal quickly because, as I've said, merged companies always take on the Cash Velocity Index of the weakest party. Equally, merging top performers can accelerate value creation far beyond anything the competition anticipates.

There is a cynical way of looking at this. If you have a company with failing Super Genba Grades, you might gain value for shareholders by seeking another company with failing grades to acquire you. Why? Because you can be certain that your target acquirer doesn't have the Super Genba due diligence system to show what your firm is really worth, and will overpay. This, basically, is what MCI did to WorldCom, what DEC did to Compaq, and what Compaq in turn did to Hewlett-Packard.

SUPER GENBA LESSONS

1. Low-cash velocity companies are in no position to make acquisitions; high-cash velocity companies usually don't need them but are the only companies that can make them accretive.

2. It is not combined market share that makes or breaks acquisition value. It is the relative Cash Velocity Indices.

3. Failure to track the right cash velocity data gives the wrong answers about you and it also gives the wrong answers about your acquisition target.

4. An acquirer's inability to convert customer information into cash at the rate of a Super Genba company overwhelms all other acquisition synergies, whatever they may be.

SUPER GENBA STEP TEN: MANAGE CUSTOMER SERVICE

One of the biggest problems in business is not so much how to manage customer service, but what to manage. Apple, for example, stays connected with its customers twenty-four hours a day through cloud interfaces on its devices. These give the firm a constant stream of information about customer activities and needs. It can adjust what it does for customers in real time. I know of no Japanese company that sells a TV, for example, the same way.

Here's how this works financially. Apple offers Apple Care and I pay for it willingly even though I know that I am unlikely to need the service. But, when I buy a Japanese TV—and I buy only Panasonic TVs—I never pay for the extended warranty. Why? Because even though I am equally convinced that I don't need the service, I also know that the distributor from whom I bought the product does not have the expertise to help me, no matter how much I pay. I also know that because of the distributor intermediary, Panasonic does not know who I am, let alone what should be done to improve my experience of Panasonic's TV.

As a result, Apple sells well-differentiated products at a premium and gets a strong flow of additional Apple Care and app revenues that endure for years. Its Japanese competition sells commodity TVs at a discount. Our family constantly upgrades all our Apple products—now four iMacs, three MacBooks, an iPad, and several iPhones, hardware and software—to the latest versions and has done so through many generations of Apple products since 1988. In that period we may have bought three TVs.

By 1988, then, Apple's *genba* was already bigger than anything available from its Japanese competition. Nothing has changed in the quarter century since. You can also see from this example how Apple connects ever-higher volumes of customer information to its ability to convert that information into cash. Panasonic may have seen, after paying its distributors, two or three thousand dollars from me during the last quarter century. Apple? At least $50,000. Probably more. And no distributor costs, every cent directly to Apple.

What if the *genba* of Japanese companies had kept expanding a quarter century ago, bringing in increasing amounts of customer information as the cost of information fell? I have no doubt whatever that the country that developed the department store and futures trading would have created innovative customer services that would be world-beating today. Japanese companies would be raking in Apple-sized profits from all corners of the globe in industry after industry. China, which for *raisons d'etat* must restrict the rate of Cloud Inflation, would be stuck selling low-margin, service-free, commodities. We would not be talking about a lost generation.

Instead, with the weakest possible *genba* Japan is competing head-to-head with China on price, a disaster.

Good customer service is not just about getting a good CRM software package, having great call centers, or offering the best warranty. It is about having a *genba* big enough to bring in competitive volumes of customer information fast enough to turn that information into cash quickly.

Eisuke Tsuyuzaki, the former CTO of Panasonic's North American operations, thinks that a cause of Japan's customer service deficiency in overseas markets is linguistic. Eisuke speaks Japanese, of course, and like me speaks English and French. So he is extra aware of subtle problems in translation. The Japanese, he says, tend to think of the word service as meaning something that is free. This creates a bias against adding services because it means increasing SG&A for no reward, something no one wants to do in any business, anywhere.

The idea that customer service is a revenue generator that creates a brand premium that cuts SG&A is, Eisuke feels, poorly understood in Japan. That is why I have created an entire Super Genba system designed to obviate as many linguistic problems as possible. Once the system generates valuable customer information, what to do with it profitably will be easier to identify and manage.

What you must never, never do, is create customer service in a vacuum. There is no point in saying, "We must have a CRM, so let's go get one." Customers must be understood in detail first.

I advise companies to think of every part of the Super Genba customer interface as a point of customer service. For example, the Global Account Management structure that I described in *Super Genba* Step Two both eliminates problems before they occur and shows where to add profitable services. More importantly, it shows how to add those services.

Nitto Denko's manufacturing innovation of integrating its operations with those of its customers is really a customer service innovation that has the effect of accelerating cash cycles for both Nitto and its customers. If Nitto thought no farther than how to ship products faster and cheaper, it could not have had these profitable relationships. Nor would it be in a position to identify additional opportunities far into the future. Its *genba* would have been too small. In a Super Genba world, customer information flowing on a well-structured customer service platform is the center of profitable scalability.

If you go back to my example of selling cash velocity, you will see that this is nothing more than a high value service relationship that drives sales, what I called a product-service hybrid in 1996.[58] Dell's great genius in the mid-1990s was to understand that if it used IT to integrate its ordering, manufacturing, and delivery systems with customers in real

---

[58] *Competing in Moore Time, Part II*, North River Ventures LLC, August 1996

time, it could deliver customized computers in a 48-hour period. By seeing its manufacturing system as including delivery right to your door, it created one of the first Hyper Monozukuri product-service hybrids.

For many years I tried, without success, to explain to my Japanese friends that Dell's use of the Internet to integrate order entry and delivery in one seamless manufacturing system was revolutionary. Dell's servers took in customer payment on the Internet, and in the same second instructed the lines on what to produce, where to ship it, how, and when. The impact on Dell's working capital was miraculous: It got paid long before it incurred an expense.

Apple took this system and tied it to a much broader product platform than Dell, creating yet higher levels of customer service. Where Dell created a product-service hybrid, Apple added a third dimension: cloud-based apps of all kinds. Today, as Samsung has found, to get the most out of a TV, you have to use an Apple interface. In other words, not even TV market world leader Samsung is in a position to control its customers' experience of its TVs. That is a customer service disaster that you do not want to repeat.

SUPER GENBA LESSONS

- Super Genba customer service is a function of operational integration with your customers, whether they are consumers or businesses.
- Operational integration Super Genba style can be an excellent source of revenues and a way to lock in customers for decades, sharply dropping the cost of gaining new customers.

CONCLUSION

As I have repeated endlessly throughout this book, everything in business follows from one maxim: The purpose of business is to turn customer information into cash faster than the competition can. Future Creators win this race. Others get left in the dust. They become the detritus of business history.

Becoming a Future Creator in a world where the *genba* expands to supersize at the rate of Cloud Inflation is the primary challenge to business success today. It was the failure of Japanese business to recognize the impact of Cloud Inflation on their markets that has swept so many great names from the world stage, relegating them to bit part roles in their markets.

Regaining global competitiveness after these decades of increasing marginalization means adapting fast to the hard realities of operating at cloud scale.

To do this, you must act on several fronts quickly and simultaneously to supersize your *genba* to accelerate Cash and Capital Velocity indices to A Grade:

1. Build the cloud into your business model
2. Build Global Account Management sales operations
3. Design real time customer information into all innovation
4. Collocate manufacturing with customers
5. Gain global Brand Superiority at cloud scale
6. Incorporate women and non-Japanese into management to cut the risks of failure
7. Globalize your organization structure on the cloud
8. Take the Big Data high ground
9. Make M&A accretive by ensuring compatible Cash Velocity Indices
10. Build world-beating cloud-based customer service

Do all these simultaneously and you will scale profitably for decades.

I am often asked which of my *Super Genba* actions is the most important. The answer is, they are all priorities and none can be taken alone or before the others. From an investor vantage point two things mark Super Genba progress: the Cash and Capital Velocity Indices and the incorporation of women and non-Japanese in top operating roles. You can get this information from business web sites like *The Wall Street Journal* and *Yahoo*.

Nowhere is it written that all Japanese companies will change all at once any more than all EU or U.S. companies changed all at once. We have seen the opposite: There are successes and failures all over the world. But, if you do not see massive, immediate shifts in at least ten top Japanese brands, you can assume the worst. Japan will not emerge from the lost generation following the Nikkei Crash of 1989. The result will be dire.

You can see here what must be done and how Nitto Denko has already done it. Which means that you can too. Today, Nitto moves quickly not so much because it has to—everyone has to—but because it can, and that gives it its critical competitive edge.

CEOs everywhere need to move forward in the same way.

You must identify the sales-doubling scale drivers used by Super Genba companies that are creating the future in the Zetabyte Era. These Future Creators use cloud scalars to suck all the air out of your markets, to scale profitably and fast on your customers, and to create markets that your customers see and you don't.

Whether your start line is $1 billion or $100 billion, my management grading system gauges your ability to become a Future Creator, to make your sales-doubling top line initiatives and innovations accretive.

If you do not get an A Grade, no amount of innovation and no number of top line initiatives, cloud or no cloud, will scale profitably. You will not create the future. Instead you will get run over by it. Don't go there!

I also set out to solve a linguistic problem: how to move Japanese companies into the business of educating customers without actually saying the words customer education. *Super Genba* was written to obviate this problem with an ecosystem-wide solution to company purpose, structure, and management. To succeed in the cloud era, companies must educate their customers and re-educate them every day. Failure cedes all the best markets to others. Allowing a linguistic problem to enable this failure would be a tragedy with geopolitical consequences. A strong, vibrant Japan is essential to a prosperous world order. *Super Genba* is the pathway to that Japan.

Then there is China, which is both a threat and an opportunity. As a matter of state policy, China wants to control all of what it sees as the markets of the future, especially automotive, computing, aviation, space, eco, and medical markets. Also as a matter of policy, it will use Party-owned companies, banks, quasi banks, distributors, and other institutions to achieve its goals, no matter the cost. This makes China a potent threat.

Anyone who tries to compete with China head-to-head using an obsolete *monozukuri* model will fail. China will use all of its state resources to bleed *monozukuri* competitors to death.

In the Party's view, failure to win this battle means the collapse of a Party-centric China where the center of the "center of all nations" (what the word China means) implodes. This will be a dynasty-ending event. The cadres will do everything in their power to prevent such an outcome.

The cloud, like the Gutenberg Press, is the Party's dynasty-ending event because it eliminates the center that the Party occupies and from which it controls the nation. Thus, the

Party will use every tool it can find to limit the rate of Cloud Inflation.[59]

Ironically, this means that the Party will forcibly deprive Chinese industry of the cloud tools it needs to achieve Super Genba and scalable profitability. Which in turn limits all China's growth avenues in all its target markets, without exception. Looked at from the perspective of *Super Genba*, China is in a lose-lose position of its own making. Without shifting to the Party-consuming cloud, China has no future. This makes China an opportunity.

Whatever dissatisfaction the Japanese, like the rest of us, may have with their own democracy, unlike China, there is no state policy preventing Japanese companies from supersizing their *genba* operations, achieving Hyper Monozukuri, gaining *kizuna* with the best customers worldwide, and stealing all China's future markets.

The only thing that Japanese businesses have to do to create the future is to decide to use *Super Genba* in its entirety. A simple yes or no. There is nothing standing in their way.

For Japan, then, the choice is simple. Stick to the old ways and become a Chinese feudatory in an Asian ecosystem stuck in a *monozukuri* tailspin. Or, supersize your *genba* and take the profitable Hyper Monozukuri markets of the future.

Panasonic is, for me, the most painful example of how all this can go wrong and how fast it can go wrong. People ask me constantly, what happened to Panasonic? Can it be saved? You were an insider. You wrote the book. You must know.

I do know and here is the answer.

---

[59] Saint-Paul, Patrick. "En Chine, Xi Jinping Déclare La Guerre Aux Blogueurs," *Le Figaro*, September 5, 2013

The story is simple enough to tell. In *Panasonic*, Kirk Nakamura and I laid out the script for the company's future. Central to our idea was to leverage the company's relentless focus on its founder, Konosuke Matsushita, by reinterpreting his thoughts for the 21st century. I did this by taking the core of his business model—the elimination of cash wait states— and using my cash velocity system to explain Konosuke in a way that managers at Panasonic and elsewhere could easily understand.

While Konosuke was a genius—it took until Steve Jobs for someone to build a company as big in a single lifetime and Jobs did not have to deal with the 1921 Crash, the deepest ever known, the 1929 Great Depression, and World War Two and its consequences—he was uneducated. His many volumes on business practices wander all over the place. They are not organized coherently. They do not start from first principles Lafley-style and built up from there.

Because of this incoherence, Konosuke's legacy was constantly misinterpreted and history shows just how easy it was for the company to run off in the wrong direction, even several dozen wrong directions.

My mission in *Panasonic* was to define Konosuke's core operating principle, make it clear to everyone, show its benefits, and the risks of failing to use it. Long before Tim Cook, Konosuke believed that the irreducible first principle of business was eliminating cash wait states. All the rest, he was convinced, would follow. In other words, like Kirk and me, he believed that cash velocity is destiny.

Communicating this to the people of Panasonic in the 21st century was central to our mission and, after a detailed introductory chapter on Konosuke, I referred back to him throughout the text. We thought that if people grasped only Konosuke's core cash velocity thinking and stuck to it, the ship would right itself and keep righting itself regardless of market conditions.

194

Kirk considered my cash velocity model so important to the company's ability to become a Future Creator that he asked me if I could make it at least half the book. I felt that we should devote more space to the rest of the restructuring team and he acquiesced. Still, it took up 45 pages, enough to make quite clear what the company had to do.

Nonetheless, I was sufficiently concerned that incoming management would not follow the script we prepared for it that, at the end of *Panasonic,* I outlined five things that my cash velocity model directed Panasonic to do immediately to ensure success.[60] You can see all of *Super Genba* in this list:

- Shift its corporate culture away from manufacturing and into demand management.
    - o *Super Genba* Step Four
- Directly manage customer experience of Panasonic products.
    - o *Super Genba* Steps One, Two and Five
- Implement superior outbound logistics and inventory controls.
    - o *Super Genba* Part One
- Create deeper global account relationships.
    - o *Super Genba* Steps Two, Nine, and Ten
- Globalize operations.
    - o *Super Genba* Steps Six, Seven, and Eight

I wanted to make sure that if management did not act, it would be clear to everyone that this would not be for the lack of very carefully prepared advice with Kirk and my many decades of experience behind it.

I then cautioned that Cyberspace Inflation, or Cloud Inflation as we know it today, posed the biggest external risk to the company because it would shift the company's markets away from it in Moore Time. Slowness to act would be fatal. If the company did not move fast on my five action

[60] McInerney, Francis, *Panasonic,* St. Martins, 2007, p. 338

points, the risks to its future would increase at the rate of Cloud Inflation. With each passing year of inaction, these risks would grow exponentially.

So, job one at Panasonic was to act on the cash velocity model at very high speed. Getting to A Grade management (it had by then risen from an F to a C-) took priority over everything else, even product development.

However, it is news to no one today that Panasonic neither acted to get top grade cash and capital velocities nor implemented any of my five Super Genba action items. It became a victim of Cloud Inflation and was dealt massive and predictable setbacks.

After Kirk left the presidency, management committed an elementary business error. It launched a huge top line initiative in green technologies, including the acquisition of Sanyo, without first having in place A Grade cash and capital velocities needed to make these initiatives accretive. The result, as our carefully prepared and very public guidelines ordained, was a disaster.

One question that I cannot answer is, why? Why would the top team not pursue a path so carefully prepared? Managements frequently change directions, which is understandable. But to reject using IT to turn the balance sheet into a key management tool that finds cash and profit in a company's existing ecosystem, and makes scaling profitably into new markets infinitely easier, is senseless. And to do it knowing full well what would happen is beyond my ability to explain.

Today, that is all in the past and there is yet another generation of management, under the leadership of CEO Kaz Tsuga. The question his team faces is, can Panasonic be saved? Or, will it be the next Kodak and become an historical footnote?

That depends on a lot of things. The Tsuga team must build a Super Genba platform for future products and services all while its customers are moving away from it at the rate of Cloud Inflation. As you can see in *Super Genba,* this will be an enormous task that will have to be completed in a very short time. In the process, many of the 88 business units, no matter how they are repackaged to make them appear more manageable, will not survive. By 2012, only a tiny number, representing less than 5% of sales, made reasonable profits. Perhaps two-thirds of the rest must be sold, merged, or closed. Putting this together will require a lot of highly trained expertise. Whether or not Panasonic will survive this undertaking in anything like the shape of its former days is an open question.

All the easy things, like selling real estate, restructuring pension funds, and cost cutting, can be done fairly quickly and will show something at the bottom line. But achieving profitable scalability, returning Panasonic to where it was in 1969 in essence, is an entirely different question. Mostly because the Panasonic of 1969 did not endure, but whatever the Tsuga team does today must endure for decades.

Super Genba says that you can easily monitor Panasonic's progress on the road to survival by watching its inventory and receivable days. If these get to fifteen and twenty respectively, the signs are good. If these remain unchanged, expect nothing.

My advice to anyone reading this book is, do not reinvent these exceptionally costly and unnecessary mistakes. The price will not just be your company. It may be Japan's independence as China gets ever more powerful. *Super Genba* offers a way forward that will bring a strong and vibrant future. Take it and prosper.

This is my answer to Koji Nishigaki's long ago question.

ACKNOWLEDGEMENTS

When writing this book I constantly recalled all those who have left their mark on my thinking about Japan.

Most of those inspirational people are trans cultural. Some speak several languages; others do not. But their thinking is global and so, in that sense, we all speak the same language.

At Nitto Denko, it has been a great honor to work with the Chairman and CEO Yukio Nagira and his predecessors Masamichi Takemoto and Hideki Yamamoto. They have been vigorous in using my suggestions and I have had the opportunity to work with their teams in all Nitto lines of business, in all functions from R&D to sales, and in all the major markets worldwide in which Nitto operates.

Arthur Matsumoto runs the LS7 Corporation which helps Kansai companies sell overseas. He is a pioneer of Japanese industry, having spent seven years in Nigeria and Kenya and eighteen in the U.S. He has an unparalleled understanding of how Japan and its markets work. I have counted on Arthur's insight for nearly twenty years.

Yoko Nakamizu speaks Japanese, English, and Chinese. She sits right on top of the culture bridge between Japan and its major markets. She specializes in building global brands using the world's biggest sporting event, the Olympic Games. After four Olympiads, she has unmatched expertise. For my book *Panasonic* she suggested an end-to-end rethink that made it the success that it became.

Tsune Katsura, with whom I have traveled the globe for Nitto Denko, is one of those rare people who has enormous education in the cultures, languages, and histories of the world and whose ability to make all these work seamlessly in a modern business environment is a marvel. He frequently adds to my knowledge of U.S. and European history and culture and has brought his deep insights to my understanding of Japanese business thinking.

Hirofumi Ise of Nitto Denko has spent many long days working with me in countless meetings with managers as we have worked through the issues and challenges of making Nitto a world-beater.

Alex Vidal played a major role in my thinking. About nine years ago when still a teenager, he told his father Rudy, with whom I worked at Panasonic on solving strategic issues, "Dad, all Apple wants to do is manage your experience of entertainment." Rudy and I were trying to figure out Apple. He repeated his son's missive. The lights went on. We cracked the code. Today, I say Apple is managing your experience of the cloud. Same thing, bigger platform. Alex's single sentence has kept me way out in front of everyone on Apple for almost a decade. I used that decade-long advantage in this book.

Hiro Uchida is a truly independent spirit. Long a part of corporate Japan, he is now an investor and advisor in several parts of the world. He has the rare ability among Japanese to speak "American," with all our facial and tonal expressions. I have often counted on his ability to see how things should work and to bridge the cultural gap.

Megumi Minami's self-taught, perfect American English is so good that you would never know that you were not speaking to an American. This, with her ability to cross cultures seamlessly almost anywhere worldwide at the drop of a hat, makes Meg a force of nature. She is in international marketing at Tsurumi Manufacturing.

At the Business in Japan discussion group on Linked In, I have to thank Megumi Oyanagi who hosts a year and a half-long BIJ forum in which I have tried out many of my ideas to see which worked and which did not.

Hartwig Rüll, who I have known for many years, has provided me with many insights into the working of multinationals and has expanded my Cash Velocity Model in new and innovative ways.

I must without a doubt thank Kirk Nakamura, the retired Chairman and CEO of Panasonic. Kirk asked me to help out Panasonic during one of its most tumultuous periods when he rebuilt the company from the ground up. Kirk gave me privileged access to Panasonic, something few foreigners get in Japan. I cannot even begin to quantify what I learned.

Also, Sean White, with whom I have been in business since 1976 and whose thinking comes up time and again in *Super Genba*.

My daughter, Alexa, has carefully reviewed and edited every report and e-mail between me and my clients for five years and has been an invaluable counsel. My son Chris, whose understanding of how the App Equivalency Rule works is exceptional, was the first to point out to me in 2008 how Apple would develop its TV products and what the risks would be to my Japanese clients. My wife, Verna McLean, has been invaluable in assessing company strategies and giving me unique insights into their motivations.

I have to thank my copy editor Sally Krefting for her patience with the endless stream of Canadian that punctuates my American English even after thirty plus years.

Finally, Joe and Mitsuko Shohtoku who have had me to their home countless times. Joe was a key member of Kirk Nakamura's reform team at Panasonic and helped me greatly with my books *Panasonic* and *Making the Green Revolution*. I like to joke that their English is so good that they could tutor American Ph.D candidates preparing for their orals. Few people understand so much about how business works in so many places. Far fewer are as gracious in how they share this understanding.

www.ingramcontent.com/pod-product-compliance
Lightning Source LLC
Chambersburg PA
CBHW042147220326
41599CB00003BB/13